RAISED IN HELL

To CYRA

ENJOY! AND MAKE
a DIFFERENCE!

9/2/14

To Cyra

Enjoy! And Make
a Difference!

9/2/14

RAISED IN HELL

A non-fiction family dramedy.

*"You have no control of
the environment into
which you are born,
but you can control
how that environment
will affect you."*

DEON PRICE

iUniverse LLC
Bloomington

RAISED IN HELL
A NON-FICTION FAMILY DRAMEDY.

Edited by Starlette English
Additional Editing by Harriet Williams & Troy Hicks
Additional Quotes and content ideas by Lita Hinson
Cover design by Sara Hicks of Unearth and Empower Communities, Inc.

iUniverse books may be ordered through booksellers or by contacting:

iUniverse LLC
1663 Liberty Drive
Bloomington, IN 47403
www.iuniverse.com
1-800-Authors (1-800-288-4677)

Because of the dynamic nature of the Internet, any web addresses or links contained in this book may have changed since publication and may no longer be valid. The views expressed in this work are solely those of the author and do not necessarily reflect the views of the publisher, and the publisher hereby disclaims any responsibility for them.

Any people depicted in stock imagery provided by Thinkstock are models, and such images are being used for illustrative purposes only. Certain stock imagery © Thinkstock.

ISBN: 978-1-4917-1638-0 (sc)
ISBN: 978-1-4917-1639-7 (e)

Library of Congress Control Number: 2013921657

Printed in the United States of America.

iUniverse rev. date: 01/25/2014

CONTENTS

Acknowledgment.. vii

Foreword ix

Preface xiii

1   "Laughter is Therapy" 1
2   1968 "What did you say yo, name was?" 10
3   A shaky beginning 16
4   The Wild Wild West 21
5   "48th & Ascott" 31
6   Patty Hearst Abduction.................................. 46
7   The Life-Changing Incident 50
8   (Foster Home Carousel) 59
9   Jim Jones.. 82
10 Dr. Jeckle & Mrs. Hyde 88
11 The Joy of Outdoors 97
12 Tough Love... 104
13 Nine Months 117
14 South Park—East L.A.................................. 136
15 The Impact of Hoop Skills 142
16 Another Traumatic Turning Point................. 166
17 The 1st and 15th 179

18 Refuge on the Court 192

19 Ground Zero of the Crack Epidemic............ 202

20 Escape From L.A. 210

21 The Hoover Plaza 219

22 West Side 231

23 The Bay Area: A Nurturing Environment..... 253

24 Family full circle 260

25 Curtain Call 267

About the Author 271

ACKNOWLEDGMENT

I humbly express my appreciation for the following supporters.

My Heavenly Father; as a youth worker and advocate, this work cannot be done effectively without your blessing. I couldn't do this work without sincere Agape love for the well-being of others. You are the source of love so all that is done in the spirit of love belongs to you.

The family; my mother; Carrie Howard who is the primary inspiration for this project. My older Brothers; Ronald Henderson and Herman Roberts, as well as my Sisters, Connie Roberts-Lorick, Cherolyn Howard and Pamela Price for contributing your stories and memory that became the blue print for "Raised in Hell". My Wife & Kids; for the encouragement. Also, much appreciation for Cousin Rita the PB, your support was worth your weight in gold.

Evelyn Polk; a lifelong soldier for the well-being of children you have been a powerful influence on me and my literary contribution to exposing the challenges of family hardships and foster care

My Students; your engaging response to the stories that encompass this message was one of the main reasons that I decided to take on this project. You have inspired me to spread these life lessons to the masses.

My mentors and colleagues: Dr. Zelty Crawford, Evelyn Polk, Michael Pritchard, Wil Cason, Kevin Bracy and Larry Moody for your influence and advice.

FOREWORD

There is a saying: "If you're going through hell, don't stop; keep going."

Well that can be said both to those reading this memoir as well as of the author from whose real life experiences, the contents have been taken. Before you begin to read I implore you to get ready for the roller coaster ride of your literary adventures because you won't want to stop until you've gotten all the way through.

Whether you're an adult or youth, "villager" or professional, and whether you have ever or never before experienced poverty, family dysfunction, and/ or separation from your biological family, if you have a heart which has not waxed cold, you will smile, cry, laugh and even holler out loud as you follow the childhood journey of author, Deon Price.

Deon takes you through the life maze of 6 year old "Little Deon" as he witnesses and experiences family addiction, violence, fear, and separation, pain, rejection, and displacement; followed by the pains of confusion, sadness, depression, apathy, and hopelessness, but most of all the enduring love for and by his biological family.

As a licensed Marriage, Family and Child Therapist who has spent more than 30 years functioning in the capacity of a counselor, social worker, foster parent, and therapist to chidren and youth, the experiences depicted in this memoir by author Deon Price, gives voice to the countless children whose lives I have been and am touched by, as they have endured experiences many adults can only fathom.

So often we assess, label and pathologize the behaviors of children and youth whose hearts and voices we do not know or even seek to know— only concerned about the external behavior and appearances. It is my continual message to those who work with and care for youth, that it is generally most effective to reach and teach them through "heart work"—connecting with them at that place in their hearts where the core issues of their existence and experience lie.

It is my heart's desire that you will not only enjoy the humor through which Deon has been gifted to share his story, but that you will also be willing to feel the pain and allow that to change and/or enhance your perceptions of and interactions with children and youth who have been through, are going through, and maybe even taking you through hell. Just know and trust that if we don't stop, both they and we can come through to the "other side" not even smelling like smoke!

It is my pleasure, honor and joy to introduce readers the story of Mr. Deon Price, who is evidence that though tried through the fire, one can come through to the other side as pure gold! ☺

PREFACE

We have absolutely no control over what type of environment we are born into. We don't get to choose our family, the geographic location or the socio-economic conditions. We simply have to play with the hand that is dealt to us. You may not be able to control the environment but you can control how the environment affects you.

As a parent and a professional, experienced in the field of youth and child development, I believe in the illustration that raising a child is like baking a cake. You can bake a good cake and choose to put any type of icing for additional sweetness or artistic appearance but if you forget a key ingredient in the recipe, no matter how good the cake looks on the outside or how sweet the icing is, on the inside, something is going to be noticeably wrong with that cake. The key ingredients are, stability, discipline and nurturing gestures of love. The home, no matter what the social or economic conditions are, should be comfortable and secure for a child's emotional stability.

This is also evident to the fact that regardless of the environment, whether abundantly filled with love and affection, or near tragically unstable as in our case, it will have a vastly different effect on the individuals who experience those same conditions. Therefore, it is darn near impossible to precisely predict how a child being raised will affect his development as an adult.

However, our development as responsible adults does have a great deal of dependency on what happened or didn't happen to us as a child. As a child, nursed on the welfare system, I am an adult who maintains a healthy balance of material needs. As a former foster child, I hold dearly to the value and bond of the original family. Having no father has made me a nurturing protective parent. Having an alcoholic mother has made me a person who rarely or almost never drinks and truly understands the need for self-control and moderation. Being often neglected, undernourished and severely underprivileged has made me a man on a mission to improve the quality of life for as many children as possible, starting with my own.

My family experiences and stories have been told to many at risk youth as a tool to connect, inspire, engage and motivate them. Some names have been changed to protect the privacy of the innocent. With respect to the engaging title, there will be no atrocious acts of abuse, no tales of being forced to drink bleach, no child being sexually abused, or extreme or exaggerated acts of physical abuse. However, this is a personal testimony of a very familiar family issue of substance abuse and poverty, during a challenging time and an even more difficult location. The primary motivation however, is to inspire and empower readers to overcome family drama and perplexing conditions to improve the quality of their lives.

The countless interviews with parents, colleagues, youth, youth workers and family members, played a significant role in the material that has become part of this project. These experiences and the often humorous tone and style in which they are delivered have been a catalyst to my success as a youth service professional. Good or bad! Tragic or triumphant! There are a multitude of life lessons in our childhood experiences. This is what inspired this testimony of "Raised in Hell". The term *Hell* as used in the title is a metaphoric or symbolic term. Contrary to the traditional religious use of the term *Hell* which signifies a literal fiery, eternal grave, a condition of suffering without end, my use of the word in this context means an extremely uncomfortable and unhealthy environment.

There may be many who may relate to these experiences. There may be some who are currently suffering the same misfortune. My sincere intention is to expose the fact that there are things that we learn from our childhood experiences that could be a seed of inspiration or encouragement for others.

In my case, as well as many others, including the tragic and triumphant story of Dave Peltzers, "A Child Called It", some individuals have the fortitude to not only survive an extremely brutal, stressful or tragic childhood but excel and succeed because of it.

CHAPTER 1

"LAUGHTER IS THERAPY"

"It is said that laughter gives you the ability to laugh at things that may have caused stress, anger, or resentment. Laughter renews our senses, awaking new experiences of forgiveness." (Lita Hinson)

The "Endzone" nightclub was filled with patrons on a Tuesday night in East Oakland, California. This small but popular spot epitomizes the image of the "hood" with small time hustlers and ghetto queens representing the hip-hop, ghetto, fabulous lifestyle. As the last comedian stepped off the stage to a few displeased customers, the M.C. announced, "O.k., our next comic, from South Central Los Angeles, Deon Deon". As I approached the stage for my first discourse as a stand-up comedian, surprisingly, I was not nervous at all. Even though this was obviously a tough crowd, I knew they could relate to what I was saying and I had years of practice, so, I was sure the material was funny. Also, I had performed before crowds much larger, tougher and angrier than these folks. My day job at the time was in juvenile probation, where I counseled at risk youth, conducted prevention courses and parenting classes. My ghetto centric since of humor has been a valuable tool throughout my upbringing. With impoverished living conditions in a neighborhood filled with crack heads, an alcoholic mother, no father, multiple siblings and a gay uncle, I had plenty of material to work with.

Sure it's funny now but believe me it was a sad situation for a child. But, as my older brother would say, "It's better to laugh about it than to cry about it." And laughing, to me, was a refuge from what some would call a miserably dysfunctional home life.

To say it was a broken home was a severe understatement. "We were broke as hell." For most of my childhood we were entirely dependent on the California welfare system which meant food stamps and a very low fixed income. Needless to say we were living far from the lap of luxury. At times our meals were just enough to line the stomach. We quite often had Chicken and dumplings without the chicken. We had powdered eggs, powdered potatoes and powdered milk. Going to school every day with a bag of powdered substance, school officials thought that I was a ten year old drug dealer. "What is this? Dope?" they would ask. "No! It's my lunch!"

How much damage has my childhood upbringing done to my mental & emotional stability? The jury is still out on that. You never really know the extent of the long term effect of a hostile and unstable home life on a child. I'm a grown man with two grown sons of my own and I'm still feeling the side effects of alcoholism, poverty and a sometimes extremely difficult upbringing.

My wife recently asked me to grab the spare car keys out of her purse. As I approached the black leather handbag, I suddenly felt extremely uncomfortable and tense as I attempted to reach inside the purse. For some reason it was a real struggle for me. Sweating like a boxer, I reverted to simply picking up the entire bag to bring it to her. "Here, you get them." I said handing her the bag. Looking at me with a puzzled look, she mumbled, "What's wrong with you?"

What was wrong? I had a childhood flashback! As an eight year old, I decided to help myself to a piece of Wrigley's chewing gum that happened to be conveniently in my mom's purse. No big deal right! Wrong! Way wrong! My mother politely asked where I got the gum from. I would have been better off saying that I found it on the floor. Instead, I responded honestly, "I got it from your pur . . ." Smack! Before I could finish the sentence, I could feel my lips being detached from my face from a swift back hand. Lesson number one! Never go in a woman's purse, period. You definitely don't go into a black woman's purse. After sharing this story with my wife much later, she understood, sympathizing with my many short comings as a result of my childhood which was mainly inflicted by the direct and indirect result of an alcoholic mother.

My mother moved to Los Angeles in the early 1960s, to escape an alcoholic husband, only to become an abusive alcoholic herself. I've always heard that there were three types of drunks; a violent drunk, a crying drunk and the kind that passes out. Well, wouldn't you know it? My mother was all three. She would get full of that Russian (Kamchatka) Vodka, terrorize us by threatening to kill us, start crying and pass out. Obviously, we couldn't wait for that last part to happen. I often joked about how we never liked having real silverware in the house. Let's just say it was a safety precaution. "It's hard to stab someone to death with a plastic fork". We basically lived on paper plates and Dixie cups. In a way it was cool with us because Mommy would break up most of the dishes which meant we didn't have to wash them.

These conditions were obviously unhealthy for the proper development of a child, yet ironically it was fruitful and nontraditionally nurturing in a strange way. The unorthodox form of love that was expressed in my upbringing embodies the depth of agape love that defines true family bond and transcends all personal issues, illnesses and tragedies. The various differences that many families have in expressing love are abundantly clear in our situation.

There was very little or no physical affection. There were no kisses good night or "I love you's" as we departed, even on uncertain terms or long periods of time. There were no light hearted sticky notes left on my bathroom mirror, reminding me that someone cares. It was just accepted in our family environment as well as in many African American families that love was assumed and it was not necessary for outwardly expressions or any corny gestures. My mother would make it brutally clear when she would often say . . ."Lord knows I love ya. But I don't have to like yo ass."

This however is another fundamental flaw according to many family therapists that often results in emotional instability and social deficiency. My experience being raised without traditional love and affection was not as detrimental to my development yet I believe it had a severely damaging outcome on most of my female siblings.

My sisters, who are all very beautiful and talented in one way or the other, all have very common personality traits that I believe was inherited from my mother. Every one of them are compassionate, resourceful, extremely opinionated but also have a very sharp tongue which makes them somewhat tough to deal with. This trait has in some ways has hindered their capacity to maintain healthy relationships. It is easy to deal with someone who is passive and agreeable but a person who is very strong willed makes it lot more challenging.

As a parent and youth worker, it has become evident that the lack of a consistent and stable father figure contributes to the imbalance that leads to a distorted perspective of healthy male female relationships among girls. They tend to have little or no respect for males or become too vulnerable or promiscuous to the slightest male attention. There is much attention given to the potential problems of fatherless boys. From my observation and experience both present and past, the potential damage is just as great for fatherless girls. I advise fathers to show just as much love and attention to your daughters as you do your sons. If you spend 30 minutes playing catch with your son, bring your daughter along too. If she's too "girly" for catch and don't want to get her hands dirty, then try bike riding or some activity where you can bond and interact with her. Your presence and example of a male figure will act as a model for her future relationships with men.

If I could bottle and market what worked for my brother Ronald and I, to help people deal with the negative consequences of a fatherless and dysfunctional home environment, we would be billionaires. I do however have a simple prescription. Laugh as much as possible. Find the humor in just about every situation you are in. It does wonders for your stress level. Research has shown that laughter, regularly promotes a source of health and wellbeing. Dr. Robin Dunbar, an evolutionary psychologist at Oxford University says there are benefits in the physical act of laughing. The simple muscular exertions involved in producing the familiar laugh out loud, he said triggered an increase in endorphins, the brain chemicals known for their feel-good effect.

To this day, I attribute my tolerance for stressful situations, health and emotional stability to my sense of humor. If your mother shows up to your school, drunk with a crooked blond wig on, looking like a black Harpo Marx, you could let the embarrassment crush you, like it did my sisters, or you could have fun with it like Ronald and I. We would just hide from her until the coast was clear to escape. Hiding from the drunken version of our mother was not only necessary for our social identity but it was also fun. One of the adverse effects of the overindulgence of alcohol is that it impairs the vision and equilibrium. There were times when she would be yelling out for us. We would be standing right behind her giggling our butts off and she would never even realize it.

CHAPTER 2

1968
"WHAT DID YOU SAY YO, NAME WAS?"

What's in a name? Tiger! Beyoncé! Or, LeBron!
Who ever thought we'd ever have a president name
Barrack?

The city of Los Angeles would watch its Lakers lose to the Boston Celtics to continue its NBA dominance. The New York Jets would capture the Super bowl title and the Detroit Tigers would win the World Series. All would be over shadowed by a dark cloud of violence and civil unrest. The year 1968 would be a time of tragedy, protest and black consciousness. The triumphs and tribulations of the civil rights movement would culminate with the assassinations of Dr. Martin Luther King Jr. in Memphis Tennessee on April 4th, and Senator

Robert F. Kennedy at the Ambassador Hotel in Los Angeles on June 6th. For African Americans, these events were met with anger and hopelessness. Some manifested their frustration through rage and riots which darken the streets of several major cities. The year also included a major accomplishment for mankind as American Astronauts orbited the moon to become the first to do so. It also included a near tragic Apollo 13 space adventure as well as a boycotted and protested Olympic games in Mexico City. During the summer Olympic Games, two black Americans Tommie Smith and John Carlos, who finished 1-3 in the 200-meter race, bowed their heads and gave the raised clinched fist Black Power salute during the national anthem as a protest against racism in the U.S.

However, this historically significant year began with the birth of a 6 lbs. 3 once African American baby boy at Holy Park hospital in Los Angeles. This child was expected to be born in February or late January. Just a few hours prior, Ms. Carrie had been enjoying herself a bit extra on December 31st 1967. Her regular routine was to get as full as she could with the beverage of her choice which was called a "Screw Driver" until she would pass out which would usually happen just before midnight. The fact that she was eight months pregnant was no reason to change or adjust her party habits. This was also the way she dealt with labor pains. She went into premature labor early New Year's morning.

Due to her state of mind at this time, along with the company she was with, this premature but healthy black child would sadly be given a name that you would never consider fit for an African American boy. She would be too inebriated to give us proper names. Nowadays the Child Protective Services or social workers would have taken the child and arrested the mother. Had it not been for my older siblings, particularly the first born, my sister Connie who was 17 when I was born, I would have been cursed with this alcohol induced identity that was given to me by an intoxicated black man who happened to love old western movies.

When my brother and sisters at home received the phone call that they had a new baby brother, they were ecstatic. When they heard what he would be named, they were horrified and decided to take action. They knew my mother who was usually intoxicated during labor which in her opinion helped her through the pains of giving birth, would not be in the right frame of mind to give the child an appropriate name. In fact she is not responsible for any of the names of her nine children. Most of us were not named until a day or so after birth. Several of my siblings are actually nameless on their legal birth certificate. Boy or Girl and our last name is what appears on their birth certificates. There is just a last name. My siblings talked it over and immediately named me "Deon" once I arrived home. Regardless of what appears on my birth certificate, Deon is the name that I live by and is my legal identity.

I often encourage young people to investigate the origins of their name. Where did it came from and who gave it to them? As in my case, the origin of your name reveals family characteristics and aspects of your history. Your name, if provided by a thoughtful sober parent, could have a significant meaning and heritage that could become part of your family legacy. I have worked with young people with names like Roosevelt or Abraham with no idea about the possible historical significance or origins of where their names may have come from. I once worked with a young African American boy whose name was Jackie, his middle name was Robinson. Sadly, he had no idea where his name may have come from. I challenged him to research the history of Jackie Robinson and to share his findings with the team the next day. Although, we were a basketball team, the next day, we had a very interesting discussion on tolerance and racism. Once he learned of the history of his name, he seemed to carry himself with a bit more confidence or swagger.

The name of a child, could affect the quality of his or her life. Unfortunately, we are in a society that still judges people by the color of their skin and, yes, the sound of their name. Remember what Mr. Obama had to endure during his campaign for the oval office, due to his name. Name discrimination is still very much a part of our environment. Qualified applicants have been unfairly screened out because their name sounds too ethnic. With this in mind, I have consulted many parents who have consciously given their children names that sound more American such as Cody Wilson or Heather Anderson. On the other side of the coin, I am also familiar with a child whose parent named him "Gangsta".

Dr. Joe Marshall, author of the book "Street Soldiers" and co-founder of the Omega Boys Club in San Francisco, CA, defined the recent deterioration of African American culture as before Crack and after Crack (B.C. and A.C.). He is certainly correct, when you consider the types of names of children who were born before the mid-80s and the types of names after the mid-80s. I'm not sure of the historical significant of the Shanequa's and Daquan's which are definitely A.C. names but I am confident in the possibilities of their future. What's in a name? Tiger! Beyoncé! Or, LeBron! Who ever thought we'd ever have a president name Barrack?

I am forever grateful for my siblings for taking action on my behalf. It was bad enough growing up in the challenging conditions of poverty and being raised by an alcoholic mother. How much worse would it have been, if I also had to face the world with a name like *El Brunco*. A black kid named after a Mexican bull fighter? The Lord had mercy on me!

CHAPTER 3

A SHAKY BEGINNING
(YOU AIN'T GOTTA GO HOME BUT . . . .)

The lack of stability could have a lasting effect on a child's development which could possibly result in emotional, behavior, social and self-esteem issues.

Our living conditions were about as stable as a three legged chair. For a brief time we were living with my aunt who had four daughters of her own. My mother had a challenging relationship with her sister due to tension and animosity between them. As two very talented singers they formed a gospel group called the Metro-tones with my uncle as the pianist in the early 1960s. The group decided to remove my mother from the group reasoning that it was her drinking that was the main cause of the problem. She believed it was jealousy and the fact that she had too many children that caused the group to turn on her. She was deeply hurt by that turn of events. I believe her poor relationship with her brother and sister perpetuated her drinking habit and depression. She was very miserable at times and the vodka seemed to be her only refuge from the emotional pain. It wasn't long before the relationship between my mother and aunt had completely deteriorated.

Our immediate family history holds the tale of an event that was the turning point between them. It was winter 1969 and we were in transition so we were temporarily living with aunt and her four daughters. During a frequent get together there was an argument between mommy and aunt that was apparently escalated by the fact that they both were a bit inebriated. My mother was for lack of a better term *pissy* drunk and was louder and more violent which was the usual affect when she drank. The argument escalated to glasses being thrown and eventually my mother being physically thrown out of the apartment and pushed down the stairs. She demanded for her kids and her purse. We quickly joined her after gathering a few things. I was a small toddler at the time not yet two years old but I too was removed from the premises along with three of my siblings. The five older siblings were not present at the time.

We were out into the cold winter streets of Los Angeles late at night and under dressed. I was wrapped in a knit blanket but none of us had a jacket, sweater or anything that would keep us warm. My sister did manage to grab my mother's purse while we were leaving the apartment. We helped our staggering mother to her feet as she was hobbled by the tumble down the stairs as well as her intoxicated state.

It was a struggled for three small children to have to literally carry a baby and a grown woman, yet we made it across the street where we sat on the well-lit front porch of a church, still snuggling together to stay warm. After several minutes of absorbing the difficult reality that we were faced with, we managed to focus on finding immediate shelter by walking several blocks to the nearest motel which was on Vermont Avenue. My mother had very little cash in her purse but she knew the manager of the motel who showed us enough sympathy to give us a room for the night. This was obviously a hardship situation. After spending a night, my mother was sober enough to make temporary arrangements with another family member. The next morning we were picked up by my Grandfather.

Our unstable and homeless situation was obviously more difficult due to our family size. We were often split up, having to live with different friends or family members. The older kids were always in a different place then us younger ones. We were with whomever our mother was living with at the time until we could afford a place of our own.

The lack of stability could have a lasting influence on a child's development which could possibly result in emotional, behavior, social and self-esteem issues. I'm affected in that I cannot give a precise location as to where I grew up, which is obviously a major part of a person's personal history. I can only say, "Los Angeles". As large as L.A. is, it will take me a half hour to break down every neighborhood we lived in or moved to from Compton to downtown L.A. which made it difficult to make and maintain childhood friends. It is also disheartening as an adult when I take my children to my home town and cannot show them the neighborhood or the house where we were raised. I always admired families that have that one house that most of the family grew up in. That house is the central location for every major family event. It holds the history and heritage of generations.

We moved around so much that I can't remember the names of all the different elementary schools that I attended. My wife's side of the family has three generations that were all raised on the same street. Like most families, there are some success stories and disappointments as well. This validates the fact that you never know how a particular environment will affect the development of a child. The instability of my upbringing inspires me as a parent to insure that my children don't experience the same fate. I understand now, how critical home stability is for a child's development.

Chapter 4

The Wild Wild West

"I've always heard my mother say "I'd kill over my kids", which was confusing to me because she was always threatening to take one of us out for something as minor as raising our voice . . ."

The atmosphere in Los Angeles in the early 70s was that of an increased influx of African American families migrating from the southern states. Many uprooted to the west to escape the still racist environment in the south. With less racial tension in California, there were better job or career opportunities for African Americans. They also believed that the westerns states were a far better place to raise and educate their children. The new freedom often resulted in more frequent social events and loose conduct which lead to the abuse of alcohol or drugs.

Alcohol and drug abuse ran rampant, particularly in the low income areas of Los Angeles. Over time, we moved in the Imperial Courts projects in a section of L.A. called Watts, for most of my toddler years. There were several incidents that were notorious and unfortunate but typical for this environment.

I came very close to being a tragic casualty of the drug scene as a toddler. Unfortunately, the abuse of prescription drugs was also part of the activities in the early 70s. They were sold and distributed around social groups and at house parties. Apparently, after a party at our home, there were a few pills inadvertently dropped on the floor the night before. As a toddler, I walked around freely and stumbled upon a few small pills that apparently resembled pieces of candy. Several minutes after consuming the pills, I began having seizures and convulsions. In a panic, I was rushed to the emergency where I was treated for drug overdose. I spent several days in the hospital and was at risk of slipping into a coma. What I thought was candy was actually a dangerously high volume of sleeping pills. This incident exposed the hazardous environment that we lived in at the time.

My mother also had several acquaintances both male and female that she had occasional confrontations with. Her boyfriend at the time was a man who is also the biological father of two of my siblings. He was a well-known L.A. hustler who always drove a nice car. He was well dressed and had a slicked back "Al Sharpton like" perm.

He originally took on the title of my father but was quite the opposite. He was a person who was involved with my mother but was far from a father. A father is a protector and care taker of children whom he is responsible for. He lived such a reckless lifestyle that he put me and my brother in grave danger. Due to his hustling lifestyle, he was often around drug dealers and shady characters. With that, he was also involved in many fights and violent confrontations. One of his confrontations played out right in front of our apartment in the Imperial Courts projects. He was confronted by a man outside the door. The argument grew into a physical altercation which led to him brandishing a revolver that he carried with him regularly. As the confrontation escalated, he fired a shot from a .22 caliber revolver at the man which missed him and entered the house. The bullet luckily slightly passed my older brothers head who was carrying me at the time and lodged in the wall near the stairs. Fortunately, no one was injured but that incident revealed his character and caused a wise decision by my mother to cut ties with him for good.

Another one of my mother's unhealthy associations resulted in yet another near tragedy that devastated our family. During the early 70's, my mother's lifestyle consisted of very frequent social gatherings. A more accurate account would be, drinking parties. One of her associates resulted in another violent and near tragic incident and would forever be a part of my family history. Although, I never met this woman I had a passionate since of animosity toward her for years. According to family sources, this woman tried to kill my mother. This incident also cost my mother a six month jail sentence and a criminal record. She was a personal friend who we also lived with for a brief time. As in most cases with my mother's associates, she was also a drinking buddy.

While living in the housing projects in Watts, our apartment was basically the place to be on Saturday nights. My mother was the host and my uncle Charlie was the bouncer. Every Saturday night we had a house full of characters. Some were relatives and some were other adults who also lived in the complex. As the sun went down and guests begin to arrive, she would send us upstairs shortly after the regulars would show up. The first arrival was always my uncle Charlie who was a deputy for the LA county Sheriff's Department. He was the house party regulator. Years later, when I became an adult he explained to me that he supported having this night club like events because it was one way my mother could drink and socialize without the danger of going out in an uncontrolled environment. He would give us a few bucks and chat with us until Mommy would give us the look that meant; *Get your a** upstairs right now.* We would end up getting snacks and treats from some of the regulars and would be very content up stairs eating Cracker Jacks and watching TV. I looked forward to opening the prize inside the Cracker Jack box which was more enjoyable than some Christmas gifts that I had received.

The theme of every party was Marvin Gays, "*Got to give it up*." That record would play all night and no one seemed to mind. That particular song seemed to put everybody in a good mood. It was almost hypnotic. To this day, when I hear it, I am taken back to those moments in the early 70s. As the evening progressed, the small, mildly lit apartment would be filled with men and women drinking, smoking and dancing to Marvin.

My mother was a heavy drinker but was still a stunningly beautiful woman which meant she had the attention of several men in the neighborhood. Being an attractive woman also generated some jealousy from some of the woman. This is what is speculated to have sparked the feud between Mommy and this woman. Once Mommy was full of that Kamchatka Vodka, she would flip into this hostile, confrontational, and sometimes violent woman. She was almost uncontrollable. The only one who could settle her down was Uncle Charlie. She was so predictable once she started drinking that people would plot to have her jump on someone they didn't like. It wouldn't take much for her to snap and go off on someone when she was intoxicated.

I think some of her friends and even relatives were entertained by this.

Ironically, this woman and my mother were close at one point. As a matter of fact, we briefly lived with her for a short time prior to their critical confrontation. It was also strained when she allegedly slapped one of my sisters. I've always heard my mother say "I'd kill over my kids", which was confusing to me because she was always threatening to take one of us out for something as minor as raising our voice at her.

Fueled with a healthy dose of alcohol, the woman armed herself with a 10 inch butcher knife and decided to crash the party. Several of us heard the confrontation grow louder. It was later revealed that this woman asked to speak to my mother in the kitchen then attacked her very aggressively but somehow loss control of the knife. In the struggle, my mother gained a hold of it and stabbed the woman several times in the chest before anyone could intervene. To this day, we are not clear on what her motivation was to initiate this assault. As the scene escalated into a loud frenzy, we were ordered to stay upstairs in the room. We could hear people yelling our mothers name several times in a way that alarmed us. We knew she was involved but did not know if she was hurt or not. We begin to cry out for her but the commotion downstairs drowned out or cries.

To our relief, I heard my mothers' voice as she ran upstairs to let us know everything was alright but she was covered in blood, which made us even more hysterical. We heard the police and ambulance downstairs. An officer came up and lead my mother away in handcuffs. At the time, we were unsure why my mother was being taken away by the police and how long she would be gone. It turned out that she would be gone for six months until the case was finally reduced from attempted murder to battery based on self-defense. She was also placed on three years' probation.

During her time incarcerated, we were initially given to the state. It was difficult for one family to take in five children, so to avoid separating us, we were allowed to live with our Grandfather for the next seven months. The older kids were all in different places. This would lead to several years of inconsistency in our living arrangements.

There is no other environment that we should have complete control other than your home. If that control is lost in the home a person as vulnerable as a child could feel completely insecure. As parents, caretakers or guardians, we should make it a priority to insure that the home environment is free from violence and turmoil.

The family dynamic has changed over the years in terms of size. Although the average family is now reduced to five as appose to nine from a previous generation. The economic conditions have made it even more difficult to raise children. The skyrocketing cost of housing has also created more hardships for families with multiple children. Motivated by my own personal experience, as a youth worker, I have worked with family service agencies to help serve foster children and children of incarcerated parents. This is yet another fine example of how bad adult behavior and decisions could directly hurt the quality of life for children.

The unstable and hazardous environment could make the child more vulnerable to maladaptive behavior. Violence in the home has a tremendous effect on the children, either directly or indirectly.

The security and comfort is instantly lost and is difficult to regain. The one place where there should be peace and safety is the home. The home should be a comfortable and secure environment. When you think about it the home is one of the few environments that we actually have control over. The outside world is brutal, stressful, unpredictable and dangerous. The home should be the one place of refuge from the ills and instability of our society.

CHAPTER 5

"48TH & ASCOTT"

"We didn't worry about gangs, cause we were living with the biggest Gangsta in L.A, Carrie Mae"

The earliest and most vivid memories that set the tone of my development was at age five. We lived in a low to mid-income area in South Central Los Angeles on 48th & Ascott. This street, as well as the house we lived in, would be a significant fixture in my life due to the traumatic events that would occur there. It was a three room single story white house with green trim. It had a midsized front yard with Roses and Greens planted along the sides. I remember how excited we were to move there, coming from the Nickerson Garden Housing Projects in Watts, California. Believe me! Watts had a well-earned reputation for being the place most likely to catch a beat down, and it wasn't because of the nationally televised riots in 1965. Living in the projects in Watts was true poverty for us so, needless to say, I was ecstatic about moving into a house in a somewhat nicer neighborhood. My brother Ronald, who is three years older than me, didn't share my enthusiasm about the move. In fact, he was literally in tears for having to leave his friends.

As the youngest of nine children, I was lovingly protected for the most part from my mother's drunken tirades by my older siblings. Unfortunately, there was no one there to shelter them from her wrath. However, by this time at least three of my older siblings had been able to move out into different environments, and understandably so.

One of my older brothers was unofficially adopted by a somewhat wealthy Caucasian family who lived in Santa Monica, California when he was 14 years old. He lived with them through high school and college. He would come to visit us in one of his adopted parent's vehicles. We were always impressed, due to the fact that no one in our immediate family had a driver's license or even access to a car. So when he came over, one bright afternoon and said he was taking Ronald and I to the Dodgers game, I was overjoyed. I had never been to a professional ball game before and actually, I hadn't been anywhere before.

Other than the traveling carnival and a drive-in movie every now and then, there was very few exciting childhood experiences. So hopping in this blue and white mini-station wagon with my brother on the way to Dodgers Stadium was the joy of my life at the time. I was equally as excited about the drive as I was about the game. I stuck my head completely out of the car window to let the cool L.A. breeze and smog hit my face. It was quite rare for me to be on the inside of a car, so I was savoring the moment. Ronald complained to him to make me sit back and relax. It seemed that everything I did was embarrassing to him but I didn't care. I was enjoying the moment.

Like any kid in the world, I will never forget the experience of my first big league game. I was so excited as we pulled up to the stadium, that I couldn't even get my seatbelt off. I also, remember the joy on my older brother's face as provider of this rare treat. Although, he probably had been to see the Dodgers several times by now, he knew it was our first time, so he was proud to share it with his younger brothers. From the taste of my first foot long Dodger Dog, to the smell of the diamond green grass and finally seeing my favorite players live and in person, will forever be imprinted in my memory.

We were there early enough to see our favorite players in a relaxed mode prior to the game. The most famous infield in big league history was there in the flesh; Steve Garvey, Davey Lopes, Bill Russell and Ron Cey. I'm not sure what it actually cost my older brother at the time who was a student at UCLA, but it was a priceless experience for Ronald and me.

These rare but joyful childhood experiences are what drives me as a father to fill my children as well as other children's lives with rewarding experiences. I often encourage parents, particularly young fathers to be cognizant of the fact that emotional memories are the longest lasting form of memories. As quoted by author and poet, Maya Angelou, "A person may forget what you say or forget what you do, but they will never forget how you made them feel." What are the emotional memories that a parent would prefer their child have of them? I'm not sure if he knew it at the time, but this experience was and still is one of the brightest moments of my childhood.

My oldest brother Herman was kind of in between households. He was there at times but was also living with his girlfriend. Herman was the black sheep of the family at the time. He was a rebel with a misunderstood thug reputation. Yet, his run-ins with Mommy were his biggest challenges. How'd you like to have that on your street resume? It was quite evident to us that surviving the streets of L.A. was nothing compared to living with *Carrie Mae*. Our experience with her was quite a challenge.

One late evening after Mommy's unofficial curfew was set, which meant if you weren't in by 10 you weren't getting in, Herman didn't make it. "DON'T YOU OPEN MY GOD DAMN DOW. She would yell. The lockdown was in full effect. We heard him tapping at the back window trying to get us to risk our lives by opening one of the doors to let him in. One of Mommy's rules were, that if she caught you opening the door for someone she had locked out, you would get knifed or at the very least be thrown out with them. This posed a very interesting dilemma for us who were in the comfort of our beds. We had a brother outside freezing to death in the middle of the night. How could we sleep with this on our minds? Eventually, my mother the *warden* would fall asleep and he would slip in through the back window. It seemed that we had to go through this every weekend. There was always a confrontation between Mommy and someone.

We were not sure how credible the threats from my mother were or how serious we should take them. We were, however, understandably worried about what our mother was capable of doing. We had seen, firsthand, what the ugly sides of her looks like, after she was full of that Kamchatka Vodka. Some people who did not know about here alcoholic condition, could not believe the stories that were being told about Carrie Mae.

There was a drastic difference in my mother when she was not under the influence of alcohol. She was a nurturing parent, an excellent homemaker with a charming and magnetic personality that made people gravitate toward her. She was known for having so many friends and associates from all walks of life. Her interpersonal skills and ability to put people at ease came very natural. I believe that most of her children inherited this trait. There would be an almost complete metamorphosis in her persona after a drink or two.

One of her closest friends, Mr. Johnson, cared enough to do some very nice things for us. He use to give us toys on our birthdays. He brought groceries occasionally and he even gave us a dog. It was a cute little Chihuahua that we named Chu-Chu who became part of our family. Mr. Johnson's gifts and generosity was welcomed until he did the unthinkable. He bought Mommy who was an often out of control alcoholic, a handgun. We assumed he got it for her protection but the poor man had no idea how horrifying it would be for us.

During an almost routine argument between Mommy and Herman, we urgently warned him that Johnson had given her a gun. He didn't believe us. As the confrontation escalated, she threatened to blow his brains out. He responded, "With what? You aint got no gun!" She then reached under her robe and pulled out the .22 caliber hand gun. "With this!" She fired a round right into the sofa near where he was standing. Shocked and horrified we all ran out of the house and down the street to a neighbor's house. Although it was a small caliber handgun it sounded like a cannon. Had it not been such a familiar sound in L.A. someone would have definitely called the police.

The next day, Cherolyn, my third sister, approached Mr. Johnson about the incident and why he shouldn't have given her a gun. He assured her that he would take the gun away and get rid of it. Now knowing our mother, we were not very assured. Still slightly shell shocked by the shooting in the living room, I sat on the floor pretending to play with a couple of toy army men on the coffee table. Mr. Johnson was talking to Mommy about shooting the gun in the house. He asked her to give him the gun. She said she didn't have it. "Where is it?" he asked. "I got rid of it yesterday", she responded so convincingly. He believed her but we knew different. Because, every time he would turn his back, she would flash the butt of the gun to us. After several days of living in terrifying fear, Herman slipped the gun out of her purse while she was asleep.

Working in the court criminal division and juvenile correction for 10 years also helped me understand the dangerous and often deathly combination of alcohol and weapons. The consequence of alcohol results in over aggressive and violent behavior. It definitely compounds the problem when guns and knives are added to the mix. I can only imagine what would have happened if we had more weapons around our home.

Besides, our sometimes violent Mother, we really had very little problems with fights or people in this neighborhood. As my older sister put it, "We didn't worry about gangs because we were living with the biggest Gangsta in L.A. Carrie Mae!" Who had already done time in Silver Brand prison for almost killing a woman. We were a well-liked family. People were very nice to us. They probably felt sorry for us. We were also a popular family because of my sisters. They were all very nice looking young ladies which had a two edge sword effect. On one hand, it was cool because we always had some wannabe hustler trying to impress them, who could get anything we wanted. If we needed a ride somewhere or something fixed around the house, there was always someone around to handle it. There was also an occasional *jealous bird* in the hood that would start some mess. But by now my mother had such a reputation that no one would event try to get into it with us.

One day before the start of the school year, Mommy walked us to the nearby barbershop to get a haircut. This was something my brother Ronald and I hated with a passion. It was almost like we were on death row and we were taking that final walk to the gas chamber. She would always force us to get a *Covatis*, which is a fancy word for almost bald.

Being baldheaded in the early seventies in a black neighborhood was torture. Not only did you get teased daily because the *in* thing was a big *Soul Train* afro, but you would also get slapped in the head so much until the back of your head and neck would be swollen by the end of the day. As we reached the corner shop we noticed that our regular barbershop was closed, so we took the next left up the street to another shop. As we entered the shop, my mother asked if we could be next for a haircut. After a brief and uncomfortable silence the older white man looked at us and said, "I don't cut that kind of hair". Shocked and steaming mad, she yelled, "What the f*#k do you mean, you don't cut this kinda hair? You racist motha f*#ka!". She grabbed a bottle of grease or something off of the counter and threw it at the man as we stormed out of the shop.

A similar incident happened after the school year began. After, another fresh Covatis (with a bleeding hair line), I was at school and my teacher notice some white flakes in my head which was later found to be dry scalp. Next thing I know, I was sitting in the nurses office with a white rubber cap on my head. Five minutes later, Ronald walked in with a white cap on his head as well. As we sat there looking like two aliens from the *Outer Limits,* I realized how ridiculous we looked and I started crying. The principal had called my Mother and told her that we had some sort of head lice and she need to come get us. When she arrived at the office, probably more aggravated for having to walk all the way up to the school, she snatched the cap off my head, rubbed the top of my head examining it and screamed, "this is just dry scalp! If you don't get these damn things off my kids head." She snatched the other cap off of Ronald's head, threw them both on the floor and slapped the nurse in the face. It sounded like one of those Three Stooges skits when Moe would slap the snot out of Larry for doing something stupid. She was so pissed, she didn't say a word on the way home.

After a few reconciliation meetings, we were allowed back into the school, obviously embarrassed. As in any environment, word travels fast and rumors start to spread. By now, we were the kids with the crazy Momma. I could sense that people begin to treat us different, even family members.

At family gatherings with cousins, aunts and uncles is where we were really affected by our mothers' condition.

I recall one 4th of July, we were invited, which was rare, to my uncle Charley's house for barbeque and the usual 4th activities. I remember being so excited to see my cousins. Although, we lived relatively close, we hardly visited each other, so these get-togethers were special for us. As the day of fun progressed into the anxiously awaited night, so did the casual consumption of alcohol. My siblings and I were aware that every drink my mother took, the closer we were to another embarrassing end to a good time. Before dark and before anyone could pop open a box of fireworks, Mommy was pretty *toasted* (drunk). At age 5 or 6, I was already conscious of my mother's behavior which was pretty sad. Imagine a kid being so concerned about his mother's conduct that he can't even fully play and enjoy himself.

As I halfheartedly played karate in the front yard with my cousin Andre, I heard," I don't give a f#*k" through the screen door. I immediately knew it was her voice and the playing stopped. I looked at my other siblings and we knew it was over. Ronald's head dropped with disappointment and shame as we begin to hear other people trying to calm her down. Particularly, my uncle Charlie who was always the most tolerable when it came to dealing with us. In fact, most of our few family invitations came from him and his wife Faye. I could hear his calming voice, "Now settle down, Cuzz. You're upsetting the kids". After a few more profane out bursts, she started crying out loud. By this time we were ready to leave just to end the embarrassment. Next thing we knew, she was passed out while my uncle carried her to his car. "You kids get in the car." And, just like that the fun was over. Before dark and before anyone could light a firecracker or even a sparkle, we were on our way home. As I glared out the window with tears in my eyes, I couldn't help but feel a deep animosity towards my mother, what she was, and how it effected us.

Our cousins would always ask, "What's wrong with T?" (short for Aunt) All I could say was "I don't know". I couldn't bring myself to say, "She's an out of control drunk. Somebody help us please!" At the time, I was unaware of the condition of Alcoholism. The only word I knew was "Drunk". I knew nothing about the power of its addiction and the possibility it being hereditary. All I knew was that my mother would drink this special orange juice called a "Screw Driver" every morning or whenever. Later, I learned that it was Vodka and Orange Juice. Vodka is clear. All I saw was the orange Juice, so for a while I thought it was the Orange Juice that had her acting crazy. Really, for a while I had this phobia about Orange Juice. I'd be over someone's house. They'd offer me some orange juice and I'd panic, "NO! This stuff is bad for you!" Needless to say I was damaged.

It took me a good while to get over the 4th of July incident. I knew it would be a while before we were ever invited to any family functions again. During this time and location is where I believe our immediate family loss contact and separated from the extended family. There would be little or no cook-outs, sleep overs or social visits from this point on for decades later. As an adult, I now understand how valuable extended family and friends could be for at risk children. I encourage men to make themselves available to other youth as mentors and resources for them. If there is no father present, then the uncle becomes a valuable asset to the child. Not having access to my extended family members made things a lot worse for me. This emotional separation would be extremely costly to us considering what would soon occur on 48th and Ascott.

CHAPTER 6

PATTY HEARST ABDUCTION

We watched a small army of police officers surround the house, firing hundreds of rounds and launching tear gas.

By far, one of the most eerie events that happened on 48th & Ascott was an incident that made national news. We were outside innocently playing in the front yard. Okay, we were outside throwing rocks. It was a slightly cloudy day. I had found a perfect rock—one of those white lawn rocks that people would pile in their yards to make it look like snow in South Central.

As I loaded up and prepared to let it fly (I was aiming for a gray Cadillac Seville), my mother frantically yelled, "Get inside now, right now!

They're shooting down the street!" I dropped the rock and ran inside. As I reached the porch, I could hear the crisp sound of gunfire. My mother ordered us to lie down on the floor, and then she rolled the black-and-white television from her room. I was shaking with fear as we gathered around the TV.

Apparently, this was not just a typical shootout in South Central Los Angeles because all three national stations—ABC, NBC, and CBS—were covering the incident. The Symbionese Liberation Army (SLA), a leftist militia group, had kidnapped Patricia Hearst, who was the granddaughter of a rich newspaper tycoon. This was the last stand of the sensational SLA crime saga, which included several bank robberies and kidnappings. The Patty Hearst controversy and trial would last for years. We watched a small army of police officers surround the house, firing hundreds of rounds and launching tear gas.

Eventually, the house collapsed and burned to the ground. We were not allowed outside for several days. I could still smell the faint scent of tear gas and smoke for days. This event put everything in perspective. For a good while, I mean at least a week, we had a peaceful home life. There was no drinking or angry confrontations. Later, I learned that the predominately black neighborhood was outraged at how the event unfolded, specifically the reckless actions of the L.A.P.D.. The public criticism questioned the lack of regard for the safety and property of the innocent residents. Bullets fired by the L.A.P.D. had hit several nearby homes, and some homes had been destroyed.

One has to wonder if they would have taken the same actions in Bel Air, California, or any other more affluent community. Another thing I learned is that alcoholism is stronger than political or social consciousness, black pride, or even black coffee. None of the above could overpower the desire to drink. Mommy copped herself half a pint of vodka, and after a brief sober break, everything was back to the norm for us. As I grew older and became more conscious of our history, I asked my mother what part she played in the civil rights movement and what her experience was. Her answer was simple and honest: "I was drunk! I didn't give a damn."

Had my mother not suffered from alcoholism, she may have introduced me to African American history and culture that would have enriched my desire to represent myself with a greater sense of pride.

The mild civil unrest and the aftermath of the Patty Hearst incident, did not escalate to the point of drawing enough public concern for the small community. The shootout was just a preliminary episode to a much greater family incident that would soon occur on Forty-Eighth and Ascott.

CHAPTER 7

THE LIFE-CHANGING INCIDENT

People were yelling, "Carrie Mae just stabbed her daughter." I even heard someone say, "Crazy Carrie done shot one of her kids . . ."

In spite of the drama and weird incidents, living on Forty-Eighth and Ascott was a nice home for us. It was relatively stable, and as far as I was concerned, it was the nicest place we had ever lived. Having said all that, our time there was short lived due to one incident that changed everything for the worse: my middle sister Cherolyn hooked up with one of the neighborhood thugs. He was actually a pretty cool cat nicknamed Bud. I'm not sure how he got his nickname, but to me he kind of resembled a young black Elmer Fudd. He came from a pretty large family who lived down the street from us. We used to visit each other quite often and eventually became two tight families. I remember being at their house for birthday parties and other events.

One evening, two of my older sisters and I were visiting them. We were in one of the boys' room that was shared by at least four brothers. One of them lifted up the mattress in the room and revealed a small arsenal of handguns and rifles. Still shell-shocked from seeing Mommy shoot at Herman in our living room and the violent shootout between the police and the SLA, I was understandably a little paranoid about guns. I frantically jumped up and broke out of the room and out of the house. As I fled up the street on my way back home, the Bud family's dog jumped from behind the bushes. He was a short collie who apparently had just been waiting for the opportunity to tear into me. He was tied up near the front gate but had just enough room in his chain to attack me. He bit my ankles and calves several times before I could kick him off. I hobbled in a labored jog back toward my house.

I didn't even bother to tell my mother what had happened because by then I knew what her response would have been: "That's what you get for taking your li'l narrow ass down there." She knew some of the brothers in that family were on the other side of the law and involved in dangerous activities and had warned all of us to stay away from that house. So, I simply just kept it to myself and kept my behind away from Bud's family complex. After that traumatic incident, you couldn't pay me to walk down to that house again.

Around the neighborhood "Bud" had given the family a notorious reputation, so when my sister Cherolyn dropped the bomb that she was pregnant at age 16, Mommy flipped. I recall being out side in the front yard when it all went down. First, I heard the familiar yelling and cursing from my mother. Cheryl was in a heated argument with Mommy over the issue. The argument escalated and Mommy broke a glass RC Cola bottle over the counter and began swinging it toward Cheryl's head. The next thing I saw was my sister running out of the house holding her head screaming with blood oozing between her fingers and down her forehead. It was a horrible site. Attempting to block the attack with her hand she received severe cuts to her head, hand and arm.

On what was just a beautiful bright sunny day in L.A., the incident quickly escalated into an all-out mayhem that created a dark cloud of stress and chaos on 48th & Ascott. Cheryl ran down to a neighbor's house still dripping with blood. Several neighbors on the street gathered near our house which caused a huge commotion in the street. People were yelling, "Carrie Mae just stabbed her daughter." I even heard someone say "Crazy Carrie done shot one of her kids . . ." Soon, the police were on the scene and I knew then that things would never be the same. What was a brief snap shot of at least residential stability, provided by a single mom was gone in one instant.

The police arrived and I had to watch from the front yard as they escorted my mother to the police car in handcuffs. She was still wearing her house shoes. They didn't even allow her to say anything to me. There was a female officer assigned to preoccupy us with mindless questions as they placed her in the vehicle. I watched helplessly, as the black & white L.A.P.D. squad car took my mother away. I did my best to resist but inevitably my eyes swelled with tears as the female officer sat Ronald and me down on the front porch. The officers mouth was moving and words were coming out but I didn't hear a thing she was saying. My world had just been flipped upside down in a matter of minutes. I often share the message with the young people who I mentor that, it only takes one bad decision that could cost you your life, freedom or in this case, your family.

The next turn of events are significant because they are indicative of the love determination and endurance of a family to overcome severe obstacles in order to remain together. With my mother well on her way to her second term at Silver Brand women's correctional facility, we were taken away by the police to the child protection service which was near the police station. The younger girls were taken by a female officer to a separate location. Cherolyn was now being treated at the hospital for her injuries.

My older brother Herman had made his way to the station downtown to make an effort to take us with him. With Connie in Montana in college, a brother attending U.C.L.A. and Debra in Louisiana, Herman was the next oldest sibling at 20 years old. He was under 21, had no home of his own and had just enlisted into the Army which meant that they could not grant him custody of us. He was now in the CPS/police station with Ronald and I, as they tried to contact our nearest relatives. He was given several attempts to contact one of our uncles or aunts to take us in or we would be placed in a foster home which was a terrible option from our perspective for many reasons.

During the early 1970s, being in a foster home, number one meant that you had no relatives around that could care for you in the absence of your parent. Foster homes at the time had a terrible reputation for abusing and neglecting children. These foster homes were perceived as individual warehouses for unwanted children. Moreover, the Foster Care system in Los Angeles County was severely flawed and unsophisticated. There was the constant concern of lost records and children never being reunited with their families which was what Herman feared the most which was the possibility of having his younger brothers and sisters lost in the system by being sent from home to home with little or no communication with their relatives.

After three unsuccessful attempts to get one of our relatives to take us in, he somberly hung up the phone. None of our relatives were willing or able to help us which caused an emotional wound that would take decades to heal. He nearly begged our aunt for help, promising her that he would send every dime of his allotment from the Army to her to help with financial support but still she was unwilling or unable to do anything for us.

As the receiver hit the phone base, I could read the expression on his face. We were screwed!

Up to this point I had rarely seen my older brother cry or show any type of emotion. I could feel his pain. He was powerless. He had always been one of our protectors. He shielded us from harm. At this point he could do nothing. He was a 20 year old young man who could barely provide for himself. Even if he wasn't due to leave for basic training in just a few days, there was no way the L.A. county child protective services would allow him to have custody of two young boys let alone two more girls. We were definitely on our way to the sad and uncertain world of the foster care system.

As the officer lead us away, Herman, fighting a glaze of tears, attempted to comfort us. "Don't worry Bro. when this is over I'll take ya'll to the Dodgers game".

I thought, Yeah right! At this point he never took us anywhere and hated us hanging around. That's when it hit me that we were in trouble. I had no idea where these strange people were taking us or when we would see our family again. I broke down and started crying uncontrollable as I tried to resist being taken away. It must have been equally painful for a young man to see his flesh and blood be hauled away in such a manner.

This painful separation would create an inseparable bond between us. From this point forward, Herman never gave up trying to keep this family together. Even after joining the Army not necessarily because he was patriotic but for gainful employment, he later express how painful it was to not be able to take care of his family when we needed him the most. After his term with the Army, this young man would spend the next several years of his life growing into the father figure that had been absent in our lives. Knowing he was all we had in terms of a responsible adult, forced him into maturity. His life from that point on shifted into a new direction and focus. There was no more street hustling, drinking, nor thug life style. He was completely committed on being a pillar of strength to maintain both his immediate and extended family.

After healing from her injuries, Cherolyn escaped from the foster home where she was placed. She was six months pregnant 16 years old and now homeless. She fled to Mozulla, Montana on a Greyhound bus to stay with my oldest sister Connie at Montana State University where she had a small apartment near the campus with two other roommates. At this point my mother was incarcerated, my siblings were now staying in four different states and I had no contact with my father. Somehow this drastic and near tragic event that occurred on 48th & Ascott which completely separated my family, was also the vehicle that would eventually bring us closer together emotionally.

Chapter 8

(Foster Home Carousel)

"I used to be lucky if we had milk for our cereal at home. Sometimes I use to eat my cereal with a fork. So I could save the milk for the next day"

With all due respect to the loving majority, not every foster parent is driven by agape love. What motivate some are the monthly financial benefits that are provided by the state. Foster parenting could be an admirable role to take on. The great gift of providing a stable home for a displaced, underprivileged or neglected child is an everlasting blessing. It's also a great risk to invite a stranger into your home, considering the uncertain results of an unstable and sometimes abusive childhood. The sincere desire to provide a nurturing environment for a child other than your own takes a special individual and I truly admire those who are honorably embracing the role of a foster parent. I get a little uneasy when we have family members over too long. So, I can appreciate those hearty individuals that open up their hearts and homes to care for someone else's child.

As I recall, our first experience in the dreaded Foster Care System was not what I had expected. Besides the natural discomfort of suddenly living with strangers and wondering where my mother was and when or if I'll see her again, the Bean Family was a very nice middle aged couple. They treated Ronald and me very well. I first recognized the difference in a household with a solid family structure. We had to brush our teeth and wash our face in the morning before breakfast. Oh, and there was a complete breakfast every morning. I certainly could get use to this! I used to be lucky if we had milk for our cereal at home. Sometimes I use to eat my cereal with a fork, so I could save the milk for the next day. We also had clean clothes that fit, dinner together at the same time and had to take a bath every night. Now, this new arrangement took me some getting use to. Obviously, an alcoholic mother was not going to maintain this kind of regular structure and detail. So, you can imagine a six year old boy without the necessary parental guidance was not big on personal hygiene.

I was always the dirtiest and most nappy headed kid on the block. So on my first night with the Bean family, I was quite embarrassed. I had no underwear on, my socks were filthy gray and my bath water left a ring of dirt around the tub that it had to be scrubbed out. For the first time, I became really self-conscious. Prior to that, I never cared about how dirty a child I was. Perhaps it was because in my previous environment, most of the kids were just as raggedy as I was, or partly because I actually enjoyed being dirty and filthy with rocks and dead bugs in my pockets.

This new environment was slightly uncomfortable yet nurturing and stable which made me feel cared for. Although there was a slight discomfort in the strange environment, there were moments of pleasure that had been absent in my previous family lifestyle. I remember the Bean family scheduling regular doctor visits and my actual first dentist appointment. The trip to the dentist experience was not as bad as I expected. I received a teeth cleaning a new toothbrush and a sucker.

Ronald and I stayed with the Bean family for several months until one Saturday morning my older brother Herman arrived to take us to one of our Aunts house. Although, I had never really knew who my aunt Jessie Mae was, I was excited about being with family and especially being reunited with my siblings. Herman had somehow persuaded the social worker and finally found one of our family members to show enough love to take us in until my mother was out of jail. We were ecstatic about being taken and reassigned to a home that would take all four of us, including two of my sisters.

Jessie Mae was the sister of my grandfather the Reverend Ike Stevenson. Her husband, Willie was an ex baseball player and a pretty low key guy. They both were in their late forties or early fifties. One of the first things Willie showed us was his garage which was filled with more baseball equipment than I had ever seen. I was gleaming with joy. There was all kinds of mitts at least thirty bats and countless hard balls. With me being an enthusiastic Dodgers fan at the time made this a dream come true. I could see Ronald & I imitating Ron Cey, Steve Garvey & Davey Lopes in the huge front yard. Although I liked the Bean Family, I was pleased about the changes that lead to us being reunited with my sisters. Later, I realized that each of my older siblings was working the system to keep us together. They obviously cared and understood how important true family structure is to young children. They also understood that there is a huge difference between living well with strangers verses struggling with your blood relatives. Most people that I know to this day would choose to struggle with their real family.

Although their intentions are good, organizations such as the Child Protective Services tend to force their often distorted perception of what's best for the child. Giving exception to the extremely abusive environments, removing the child from the home often creates more harm than good in the long term. In my 20 years' experience in youth & family services, I have learned that youth who are placed in Foster Homes, Group Homes or Juvenile Detention Centers with no real connection or bond with their original family, tend to be more vulnerable to negative influences and are more likely to gravitate toward criminal mischief.

At this point and time, things were going pretty well with aunt Jessie Mae. We had all enrolled in school and was receiving regular visits from other family members, mainly my adult siblings. We would get an occasional visit from my Grandfather, the Rev. Ike Stevenson who would stop by to make sure we would be in church on Sunday.

My favorite part of living with aunt Jessie Mae was the fact that she also owned a small thrift store in the neighborhood. The store also sold used clothes and candy. We had to walk to the store on the way home from school and stay there until the store closed in the evening. She had a small room in the rear of the store where we could take a nap or do homework. By sisters thought it was boring even though they sometimes got to work the register but for Ronald and I it was paradise. We had access to every type of candy there was, Abba Zabba, Snickers, Now & Laters, Red Hots, Lemon Heads and my favorite, Butter Fingers. Actually, this little store was when I first tasted a Butter Finger candy bar. Aunt Jessie Mae had them on display for 5 cents. She gave us one to taste and to keep us content while we waited. It was the absolute best thing I had ever tasted. From that point on I was addicted. I ate so many Butter Fingers that I don't think she had enough to sell. Soon we were no longer allowed in the store after school. I wonder why?

After several months living with Jessie Mae, we begin to hear a different tone in her voice toward us. That loving nurturing demeanor that made us feel at home was gone. We begin to hear her complain more about how expensive things were and how they don't pay her enough to put up with all the changes we bring. I guess what they call the *honeymoon* period was over and the reality of having four kids to take care of became more prevalent. Again, we looked at each other to see if there was something we were doing to cause problems.

One of my older sisters was 12 years old and the oldest of the four of us going through these foster home changes. She was conscious enough to sense when we were about to be moved again, urging us to stop arguing and fighting all the time. She even suggested we cut back on eating or asking for seconds at dinner. We were hoping that this would somehow prevent us from being sent to yet another home. We did what she suggested which no easy task was.

I had to be the greediest kid on the planet when it came to sweets, so to bring myself to say no thanks when someone asked me if I wanted desert was a real challenge. I was even tempted to accept a few of those nasty Peanut Butter Cookies. But when I reached out to accept the cookies, I was immediately bumped by my sister, reminding me of our agreement. I sadly declined, "No thank you". Yet my stomach was saying "Take that cookie fool". I remember taking an extreme measure to conceal my zeal for late night snacks by hiding them. I would take pieces of biscuits or bread from breakfast, lunch or dinner and tuck them away in my pocket just to have a snack before bed time. Sometimes, I would hide them in my pillow case until one day I was met with a large tribe of ants in my bed.

Our efforts to reduce food consumption and behavior modifications were all in vain. Less than a month later, Aunt Jessie Mae sat us down with tears in her eyes and told us that she could no longer keep us and the social worker was coming to take us to another place to live. This was absolutely devastating to me. Our own family didn't want us. I had never felt so worthless in my life. We were basically homeless and it seemed like no one cared.

The resiliency of this family is evident of how valuable it is to have love and faith be your driving force to overcome any obstacle. The resources that you have as a family can be a powerful cord that will not be broken. You can yank it, pull it, stretch it or burn it, but if it's bonded by love and faith, it will hold strong. No matter where we were living or who we were with, I could still feel the presence of my mother and family. I begin to believe that no matter what happened we would somehow be reunited.

I wondered where my mother was. I knew the police had taken her away but no one really explained what was going on and when or if she was coming to get us. I used to sit on the porch and watch cars go by imagining that one day one of them would stop and my mother would get out looking beautiful & sober. She would walk up immaculately dressed drawing attention from everyone on the block to take us to our new home. This reoccurring day dream would get more detail at each occurrence. I was just a kid who wanted his mommy. It didn't matter that she was a drinker and sometimes violent. I didn't care, I JUST WANTED MY MOMMY! It was beginning to have a serious emotional effect on me.

Again, our main concern was being separated. Luckily the next home we moved to was another couple who agreed to take all four of us. The Perkins folks were also middle aged and a lot stricter and reserved than the Bean family and Aunt Jessie Mae. Mrs. Perkins was the head of the household and did most of the interacting with us. She was a very firm and no nonsense type of woman. She was more like a civilian domesticated drill sergeant. I had what you would call a healthy fear of her. Not the type of life threatening fear that I had for my mother who would get full of her *sauce* and start throwing knives at my older brothers and sisters. But the type of fear you have for a mean teacher that had the power to fail you and make you repeat a grade. I knew Mrs. Perkins could have one bad experience with us and could very easily have a meeting with our social worker and have us separated again.

I literally would tremble when I would hear that the social worker is coming to visit or she would have a meeting with our social worker. Even at age six, I was aware that it was hard for people to allow one child in their home let alone four. I was also aware how lucky we were to have an older couple open their home to four kids. So I tried my best to be a good kid with hopes that my good behavior would somehow lead this family back together again. It didn't matter to me that my mother was now in the system as a violent alcoholic. Nor did it matter that we lived for the most part in poverty. What mattered was that we loved our mother regardless and we wanted to be together.

Mrs. Perkins was a very unique woman. She had some interesting qualities about her that put quite a stain on our relationship. In fact she petrified me at times. They kept a dog that was inside sometimes but was mainly kept outside. Very frequently the dog would drop a *load* on the floor in the kitchen or wherever he felt the urge. This *special* woman would pick the fresh warm moist pile of dog mess up with her bare hands and throw it away. Now of course she would immediately wash her hands thoroughly but to a kid, those hands are never clean. From the time we saw her do this we were instantly disgusted with her every touch. From that moment on,` she was no longer Mrs. Perkins, to us she was

"Boo Boo Lady". If any of us saw her touching any one of us, the others would disown that kid for life. This poor woman could not understand why we would not let her touch us even with her baby pinky throughout the year that we stayed with her. She actually thought we had some serious emotional issues or suffered physical affection deprivation. She even recommended that we see a counselor. From our point of view, she was the one who needed counseling. Anyone crazy enough to pick up dog mess with her bare hands has got to be missing a few screws in the head.

Eventually we adapted to the Perkins folks over several months. The house was a nice four room flat on the east side of Los Angeles that was built in the late 50s. There was huge front yard with a wired fence and a decent sized back yard. Ronald and I had our own room next to the girls. We were all in school and pretty much adapting to new friends and yet another neighborhood.

I begin to slightly withdraw from social interactions. I was doing a lot of wining and acting out. I begin to realize that if we were unwanted by our own family and maybe even my own mother, than eventually these people would get rid of us too, no matter how well behaved we were. It was certainly true in the last place we lived. So I begin to not care anymore. I wanted my way a lot and when I didn't get it, I would start crying or throw a mild tantrum until someone would give in. I would over hear my older siblings talking about reporting our foster parents to the social worker if we were abused or mistreated. Knowing that, I quickly realized that we probably wouldn't be getting too many whippings. I didn't fear any consequences for my behavior. I knew this strategy wouldn't work with Mommy. She had no reservations for giving one us a good butt whipping with the closest object she could find. It made no difference to her whether it was a belt, a shoe, an extension cord or a Soda bottle which is what got us into this mess.

I also begin to wonder if my mother was out trying to find us a home or if she was out of jail and had second thoughts about coming to get us at all. My fear was that she was so messed up with alcohol that she couldn't get herself together. I also wondered about my older brothers and sisters who we hadn't seen or heard from in a while. Had they given up on us? Would we ever be together as a family again? Not knowing, made my mind wonder quite often.

My curiosity was satisfied when I heard some wonderful news from Mrs. Perkins, "Tomorrow we goin to see yaws Momma". That night, I was so excited I couldn't sleep. Ronald and I wondered where she was and how she was doing. I also wondered how she looked now. It had been over a year. Even with her alcoholic condition she was always a beautiful woman with smooth fair skin and jet black hair. I could picture myself giving her a big hug. We got up very early to get dressed. We had to put on our church cloths so I knew we were going somewhere special. As we approached this huge building down town, I begin to get that same uncomfortable feeling I use to get when we had to visit our social worker.

After passing through the front lobby, I knew this was not going to be a warm fuzzy reunion with my mother who I haven't seen in a year. Anyway, I was still excited to see her in any capacity. As we arrived in our places I saw men in suites and policeman or bailiffs in the room. I realized that we were in a courtroom. As the judge took the stand

I saw two bailiffs enter the room through the rear with a person dressed in blue. I quickly realized it was mommy. Her hair was short and she looked pale. Her eyes met mine as if she didn't see anyone else in the room. The look on her face manifested both pleasure and shame as she sat shackled like an animal.

Although I was pleased to see her, I was also sad for her as I shared her pain. I wanted and needed her embrace at that moment more than ever. They wouldn't even allow me to wave at her. It was one of the most Inhuman things you could do to a child. To dangle their greatest need in their face, yet deprive them of having it. The purest and most powerful love between two human beings is that of a mother and child. To deny this was absolutely torture for me. To add salt to an open wound, they even forced me to testify. I was obviously, intimidated by this process as I sat in a large chair being interrogated. The judge kept asking me to speak up. At age 6, I was in a court room being asked questions about the worse day of my life by people who wanted to send my mother away. All along, they were saying that they were doing it for the best interest of the child. What child? Me? Or my brothers and sisters? No one asked us what we wanted. My best interest was sitting there shackled to the chair. If they really cared about my best interest they would have let me give my mother a hug and let me tell her how much I love her and miss her. They would release her and set us free even if we had nowhere to go.

That experience deeply affected me. As much as I desired to see my mother, I hated seeing her like that. It is an image that will forever taint my childhood. Under those circumstances, I was never even allowed to even speak to my mother. Unfortunately, the only way I could see her for the next several months would be in a tense and uncomfortable court room.

My inner struggles continued as I continued to withdraw. In fact, I hardly spoke to anyone. Through my hardships and family changes, I had developed low self-esteem and very poor social skills. At age seven I could barely hold a conversation even with kids my own age. The instability and lack of much needed affection resulted in me being an insecure and often depressed child.

The one constant person up to that point who gave me a little balance was Ronald, who was just three years older and always kept me from slipping into manic depression. His since of humor grew on me and incidentally became like therapy that helped soften the hardships and relieve the heartache. He always kept me on my toes by challenging me in different ways. He was just a kid himself so I know he had no idea how the teasing and sometimes bullying force me to defend myself physically and emotionally which actually improve my self-confidence. As brothers close in age, we literally grew up together. We were together almost all the time and suffered the same experiences together. There was very few times when Ronald and I were not together. We were never separated from each other. There were times during our living in foster homes when we knew that we only had each other, even if we could not be reuniting with the rest of the family.

There was a powerful unspoken bond between us even though we got on each other's nerves, pissed each other off and sometimes fought. We were inseparable. Are names were almost always spoken together. Whether we were being blamed for something or being summoned, it was always, "Where's Ronald and Deon?" "Sometime we even wore the same cloths to school at the same time. He had his arm in one side of the Jacket and I had mine in the other."

By me being constantly challenged by my slightly older brother, I was pretty well prepared for most issues that I would encounter in school or in the hood. The way I mainly handled things were simple. I would run like hell. I was always a relatively small kid. So fighting, for the most part was not an option for me at the time.

We stayed with the Perkins family for several more months until we were given the news that I had been waiting to hear for almost two years; that our mother was coming to get us soon. Those very words sent a joyful chill through my entire body. The four of us shared a rare and private emotional moment in our rooms that night. Mrs. Perkins would regret telling me this, because every day I would get up and ask her if my mother was coming today. She actually got annoyed with me and told me not to ask her that again. But that didn't stop me. I would ask one of my siblings to ask her every day until she told us that actually my older sister Connie would be coming on Saturday to pick us up.

I was so excited that I couldn't think straight. We spent most of the week packing a few items, mainly clothes. Mrs. Perkins kept trying to direct me on how to pack things into this box, but I wasn't hearing her. I couldn't care less about these, *"leave it to beaver looking clothes"*. I just couldn't wait to get the heck out of there. Not that this was a bad living experience. Actually, the Perkins made me feel more comfortable than any of the other foster homes that we stayed in. It was just that I was so tired and emotionally spent from this whole two year experience that I was just so ready to be reunited with my original family.

By Friday night, I was so anxious I couldn't sleep. I actually got up to get dressed so early that it was still dark and everyone was still asleep. As I got up to wash my face and brush my teeth, which was something that they normally had to darn near hog tie me to have done, my sister got up slightly irritated, "Boy! Go get back in the bed, it's 5 o'clock in the morning". I reluctantly returned to my room but I just continued getting dressed. Soon it was a bright sunny Saturday morning and all was well. After breakfast, I couldn't wait to get outside. I played in the yard and waited on the porch for my sister. I peered inside every car that passed by, hoping it was her. I stayed outside for hours. It was now after 12 noon and Mrs. Perkins had to force me to come in for lunch. I wolfed down the Peanut Butter & Jelly sandwich and was right back outside manning my post. Finally, I saw a small white car pull up and it was her. I ran up to the car yelling, "she's here!" I didn't even wait until she got out the car. I wanted to just hop right in and go. My other siblings were not far behind me in anxiety. Although they were a little more reserved in their expression, they were just as excited as I was to see my oldest sister.

It was almost identical to my dream of seeing my mother step out of a car to come get us. However, it was a younger version of Carrie Howard, but just as beautiful, as my big sister stepped out of the vehicle drawing attention from the neighbors. She was absolutely gorgeous with a full curly afro and a window pained designed blue jean jump suit, resembling the actress, Pam Grier. After a long group hug, we guided her inside.

Our last goodbyes to Mrs. Perkins was a blur. Although her hospitality was well appreciated, it was obvious that we did not want to let another minute delay our reunion with our mother. I believe she understood that, because she was the first to say, "I know ya'll excited to go see ya Momma. Ya'll gone on and be good now." Either that or she was just as eager to get rid of four hard headed ghetto Children. At any rate, it was music to my ears.

As we piled our stuff in that small white car and drove off, I felt a chill of excitement and anxiety run through my body. At the moment I had no idea where we were headed nor did I care. I didn't set any unrealistic expectations of us living in a large brand new house in Malibu, with a pool. Even at 7 years old I had enough sense to know that a Black female ex-convict who was also an Alcoholic could not obtain such a luxury. During the ride, Connie filled us in on our new living arrangements in the city of Compton.

We were actually going to live with my Great Grandfather, Poppa and Uncle Fred. We were never really that close to any of our relatives due to the distance that separated us because of my mother's reputation as a heavy drinker. Because of this, I barely knew this precious beloved old man that everyone knew as, Poppa.

My grandmother had passed away before I was born and my grandfather Ike Stevenson was a fast lane Baptist Minister with a mean streak. So I never experienced the nurturing of having a grandparent to spoil me and sit around and share old family stories with. I always heard family members refer to Poppa but nothing specific. There were always detailed stories about our notorious relatives. There were funny stories, jail stories, the thieves the womanizers, but there was never anything outstanding about Poppa, which means he was probably a pretty cool and stable old fellow. By this time he was over eighty years old and could barely speak. He lived in a four bedroom house with Uncle Fred who was up in age as well, so it made since to have family move in with them as caretakers. Also, it was a blessing to us because there was enough room for all of us, even Connie and her little son Aamkul.

As we pulled up to this brown flat with a well-cared for front yard in what seemed to be a nice neighborhood, I saw my mother standing on the front porch. "Here are my Babies!" she yelled. She was wearing an auburn top with some blue bellbottom jeans. We quickly piled out of the vehicle to meet her at the side walk. I made sure I was the first one to reach her. It was a very emotional moment that no one seemed to mind. There is a classic Polaroid photo of that moment that exists. It is now weather beaten, faded and slightly torn but still depicts the emotional clarity of that moment as clear as HD TV. As we ended our embrace, I noticed more unfamiliar individuals now standing near the front door. Those individuals would be introduced to me as my uncle Fred, my Great Grandfather & Mrs. Saundra. They had prepared a much anticipated mini home coming party for us. Finally, after two years and three months, we were reunited again as a family.

I am forever grateful for my older siblings for not giving up on us and allowing us to be maneuvered through the inferior foster care system. The emotional damage that is caused by family abandonment could cause lifelong issues for a child.

Chapter 9

Jim Jones

"Less than three years later, we would be shocked to be watching the national news reports of a massive suicide by members of the Peoples Temple"

One of the most shocking and tragic events that occurred involving united states citizens, would occur in South America. The horrific Guyana Tragedy would be orchestrated by Reverend Jim Jones. The religious cult, entitled the People Temples nearly completely consumed my mother's life in the mid-seventies.

Jim Jones was the American founder of the Peoples Temple, which became synonymous with group suicide after the November 18, 1978 mass murder-suicide in their isolated agricultural intentional community called Jonestown, located in Guyana, South America. Over 900 people died from cyanide poisoning or gunshot wounds. To the extent the actions in Jonestown were viewed as a mass suicide, it is one of the largest such mass suicides in history, perhaps the largest in over 1,900 years and the largest mass suicide of United States citizens. At a nearby airstrip, the event also resulted in the first and only murder of a U.S. Congressman, Leo Ryan, in the line of duty in the history of the United States, along with the murder of three journalists and a defecting temple member.

After twenty years in the Baptist church of our grandfather, my mother was overwhelmed by the powerful, influence and preaching of Mr. Jim Jones. As a young child, I can recall attending The Church Services of Jim Jones when his congregation was in the Los Angeles area. We were able to recite the popular Sunday school song, "Welcome, welcome every one . . . ." It was often a well anticipated event attending The Peoples Temple. Attending was not an option for us just as it was not an option for us to attend church when we lived with our grandfather Rev. Ike Stevenson. Although the church service at the Peoples Temple was unbearably long, I actually enjoyed the free lunch that was provided midway through the service. Jim Jones appeared to be a very personable and passionate man. I recall meeting him for the first time while my mother was preparing to sing in the Peoples Temple choir. He would gently hold the back of my head when he spoke to me as if he was delivering some sort of power or energy. Weird dude!

One of the weirdest experiences I encountered with Mr. Jones was after my nephew was born. My mother brought him to the Peoples Temple for a blessing. She persuaded my sister to allow her to have her grandson blessed by who she believed was a special Reverend who was both a prophet and a healer. Jim Jones dipped his hand in what he described as holy water and gently rubbed the child's forehead with his finger in the form of a cross. Ironically, that same location on my nephews' forehead would soon be replaced by several stitches from a freak accident less than two years later.

Jones was very popular among African American people. He was widely respected for setting up a racially mixed church which helped the disadvantaged. His congregation was 68 percent African American.

My mother was so caught up in his congregation that she wore a medallion of him around her neck faithfully. Although her enthusiasm and loyalty for Rev. Jones lead her to reduce her alcohol consumption, it was also beginning to wear on the family. It became an obsession. There were pictures of him all over the house as if he were of divine origin. She even replaced a popular painted picture of the accepted blond haired blue eyed depiction of Jesus with the sunglass wearing Minister Jim Jones. Sadly, she would have faithfully followed Jim Jones anywhere, even to a remote location in South America.

Jones was just beginning to preach, organize and campaign for his movement or mass exodus as he called it to an independent cultural and spiritual society outside of the United States. He was also strategically planning to flee to avoid growing accusations of child molestation and corruption within the Peoples Temple at the time.

Fortunately or unfortunately depending on your perspective, Jim Jones would do an unthinkable gesture for anyone, particularly a minister that would snap my mother out of it and force her to begin to shy away from Mr. Jim Jones and the peoples temple. During one of his sermons he often criticized the bible and at times challenged its accuracy. This particular afternoon he took his criticism of the bible to another level as he ripped a page out of the King James Version of the Bible and balled it up to discard it. Some have even claimed that they witnessed him making an obscene gesture with that page prior to throwing it aside.

Whatever he did on that day was enough to turn quite a few people including my mother away from his congregation which ultimately probably save her and maybe my life. Had it not been for that incident, she would have more than likely followed Jim Jones and many of her friends to the Jungles of Guyana. Many of the followers were convinced to forfeit or sale their homes and assets to support the Peoples Temple movement to Guyana.

Although we had no home or assets, my mother was so well connected with Jim Jones's congregation that she would have been invited anyway.

Less than three years later we would be shocked to be watching the national news reports of a massive suicide by members of the Peoples Temple. As I watched the live footage of the tragedy on the news and saw the countless rows of lifeless bodies of men woman and children, I recalled getting chills with a pinching ache in my stomach. It was an eerie sickening feeling that I had never felt or would ever experience again to this day. For years later, I would have nightmares as a result of my experience and connection with such a horrible event. Even the mention of his name, the Peoples Temple or that awful child's song "Welcome, Everyone" played like a dreaded horror film to me.

CHAPTER 10

DR. JECKLE & MRS. HYDE

"She would never get us the complete gift. She would get me the handle bars for Christmas the tires on my birthday, I'd get a different part every year. I didn't have a whole bike until I was 19 years old."

I believe the old horror stories of Dr. Jeckle & Mr. Hyde was inspired by Alcoholism. The basic premise of this story is exactly like my mother when she would consume the dreadful potion (vodka) and turn almost instantly into this feared monster of a woman. Her facial expression would change. It was like she would do a complete metamorphosis. Without it, she was for the most part a sweet nurturing parent. We had quality moments that gave us a snapshot of normalcy. However, all too often the ugly side or Mrs. Hyde would appear. One minute we were a poor version of the Brady Bunch(without the father & the big house). The next minute it's the Creature Feature.

Alcoholism and drugs relentlessly attacks the fiber of the family by first destroying their self-control and sense of responsibility. A parent who is under siege by the vices of chemical dependency has no bearing on his or her priorities. A seriously ill alcoholic would not discern what the detrimental effect is to their child's emotional and social wellbeing. How damaging it is for a child to experience their parent staggering down the street obviously under the influence?

My mother showed up to a parent teacher conference wreaking with vodka. Obviously, I was the joke of 95th Street Elementary for the entire school year. Kids are brutally insensitive. Even people who were my friends shared a private joke on me whenever the subject of mothers surfaced. Did she realize how much her thoughtless actions affected me?

I recall a rare moment when we were showered with all kinds of Christmas gifts from one of her boyfriends at the time. We were overwhelmed with joy, being severely under privileged as we were. "My mother was so cheap she would never get us the complete gift. She would get me the handle bars for Christmas the tires on my birthday, I'd get a different part every year. I didn't have a whole bike until I was 19 years old." So to have this many presents to open was unreal for us. There were Hot Wheels, Race Tracks, Tonka Toys, GI Joe action figures and even Barbie dolls for my sisters. We were really having a great family moment.

Until . . . She must have briefly slipped into the kitchen to have a cup of eggnog obviously spiked with her beverage of choice. I was preoccupied with our new gifts to notice that the generous gentleman had changed clothes and was prepared to leave. This infuriated my mother. And just like that, she changed from an appreciative mother to a hostile combatant. She cursed this man out so loud we knew we had to retreat to the other room. Suddenly, I heard the door slam and the man was gone. There was a brief silence. I begin to calm down a bit thinking that maybe she would settle down and we can go back to enjoying our new presents. As we re-entered the room we saw her open the living room window and yell down to the man. ". . . . and you can take back these G** Damn Toys . . ." We watched in horror as she threw every toy down to the busy street from our fourth floor window. I almost got the nerve to try and stop her but thought against it. All I could do was stand there and cry as the toys of my dreams were being shattered and ran over by oncoming traffic. It was *almost* a great Christmas.

Prior to that moment Ronald and I would spend hours looking through the huge toy section of the Sears catalog, just dreaming of someday having some of those wonderful toys. Well, that day came and went in a matter of an hour. Easy come, Easy Go! It took me a while to get over that. I was truly hurt and extremely disappointed. This experience was worse than not having the things you desire. Having these wonderful gifts for brief moment and then having them destroyed right before your eyes was beyond emotional abuse; it was cruel.

This sickness that my mother possessed obviously took away all rational thinking. If she would have any remorse from her behavior while under the influence I never saw it. My older brothers and sister would sometimes find her stash of vodka and hide it or get rid of it. This was extremely dangerous, particularly when she was younger and much stronger. There were times when she would actually chase my older siblings with harmful intent. I recall my older brother reminiscing about playing marbles with his friends. His young friend looked up pointing "Hay man isn't that your mother & your sister running down the street?" obviously embarrassed, he'd deny it. "Nope, I don't know those people".

It would really get interesting when my older brothers would find the nerve to take it a step further and actually put water in one of her vodka bottles. Now if you ever want to really start some mess, this would be number one on the top 10 ways to piss off an alcoholic. Now, if you live with an alcoholic I wouldn't try this at home. What they would do is find her stash and pour out whatever was left in the bottle and refill it with water to the same level as they found it. With the naked eye, you can't tell the difference between vodka and faucet water. They would place the tampered bottle back where they found it and wait for the action to start. The fun part was when she would get her mind and taste buds set only to get the unpleasant but pure surprise of faucet water. Sometimes, I would get a ring side seat just to see her take that bottle and shatter it against the wall into a million pieces.

I was always never suspected because I was too young to be so conniving and cruel, yet I did participate in the act sometimes. However, my older brother Ronald who was always the blame had to get a safe distance. After a brief tirade of profanities, she would creep off to the liquor store for a new half of pint of Kamchatka. Unfortunately, this was one of the ways we dealt with the situation. We had to find the humor in a sometimes horrid environment. There was no counseling available for us. As a matter of fact we never even spoke of our mother's condition outside the immediate family. It was sort of an unwritten code that you never talked about family issues to any one out side of the house no matter how bad things were.

Considering what we had already been through as a family up until that point, we were certainly capable of surviving this. We absolutely had loss all trust in the L.A. County Family Services, The Child Protective Services and especially the Los Angeles Police Department. We had even gave up on the possibility of getting help from extended family members such as Aunts & Uncles. Even our Grandfather the Preacher, seemed to be unapproachable if we needed help. It was clear that no one wanted to be bothered with Carrie Mae or her kids. And we certainly didn't want to do or say anything that would lead us back into that dreadful foster home system. We were definitely on our own with no one to talk to or for some encouragement. Our only therapy was laughter.

Due to our hardship conditions, compounded by my mother's alcoholism, we were often short on basic needs supplies and food. Quite often we had to intervene by stealing money from our mother's purse to purchase food or to pay bills. Obviously, this act of survival created a tremendous amount of domestic drama and sometimes violence. There were several times when the police were called after one of my older siblings was discovered to have taken the funds. Regardless of what necessities were purchased with the money it was still considered a criminal act in the eyes of the L.A.P.D. Most of the time when the police were involved they could see my mother's intoxicated state and simply ignored her accusations. With no arrest, instant conviction or execution by firing range which was what she demanded from the PD, all hell would break lose for the remainder of the night.

I would often walk with my mother to the store to get household items and sometimes food. I enjoyed the walk with her mainly because she would buy me a pack of Now & Laters or Lemon Heads. She was always a very popular woman no matter where we lived. She had a presence and a warm personality that made people gravitate toward her. As we approached the store there were probably seven or eight different people that would greet us along the way.

There were those brief moments that made me feel proud that she was my mother. That feeling would change almost immediately once we got to the checkout counter to pay for our grocery. As the checker would begin to bag the items he would ask. "Would that be all Ms. Carrie?" She would then utter the words that would haunt me for years. "Give me a half of Pint of Kamchatka". To the average 7 year old, this meant nothing but to me it meant there was going to be hell tonight. I would often pray that they would run out of alcohol or that at least there would be no more Vodka today. *In the neighborhood we lived in, there was a liquor store on every block and they would run out of Milk, Sugar, Bread, anything but they never ever ran out of Liquor.* As a result, alcohol and drugs completely saturated our community as it does in most urban communities to this day.

CHAPTER 11

THE JOY OF OUTDOORS

"I use to have to eat chicken and dumplings without the chicken. By the time I got my share, the only thing left would be soup & bones."

Like most kids growing up in the 70s, I absolutely enjoyed being outside all the time. In Southern California, the weather was perfectly suitable for a kid who loved the great outdoors. The activities were primitive but cultivated the creative and artistic development of a child. We played with joy, hide and seek, freeze tag, street football, and when we really felt daring; Ding Dong ditch which was the formal name. Since most people in the *hood* didn't have sophisticated door bells we would just knock on someone's door and run. Most residents in our hood didn't even have a peep hole. We didn't have a peep hole but we had a bullet hole that was never repaired. We would exhaust every option of outdoor excitement only going inside to eat or relieve ourselves. Some of us didn't even go in for that. When nature called we would find a tree or escape behind a building.

As my playmates begin to retreat to their perspective homes, quite often we would smell the warm homely cent of fresh fried chicken. We would proudly debate over whose mother was responsible for the enticing aroma. I'd play along and throw my voice into the action, that's my mommas cooking" knowing damn well how unlikely it would be coming from my house. I'd be lucky if we had third day leftovers. "I use to have to eat chicken and dumplings without the chicken. By the time I got my share, the only thing left would be soup & bones." At this point in her condition, my mother had lost her desire to prepare meals regularly. That responsibility was delegated to my older sisters if they were around. In an apartment complex or housing project we inevitably shared aromas and sounds with the neighbors among other things. I remember going next door to borrow peanut butter, upstairs to borrow jelly and down stairs to borrow some bread to complete a Peanut Butter and Jelly sandwich.

As the evening approached I would began to realize my joy would soon turn to fear and stress. Most kids hated being called inside but my hatred for going home was real. I truly feared what the night would bring. Although I despised it most of the time I'd have to go home to an uncertain situation. As I would approach home I'd be a little uneasy about what would be on the other side of the door. One of my mother's most regular acts of alcohol induced emotional abuse was to force us to turn off every light in the house as night time approached. I would have to sit uncomfortably in pitch black darkness for hours obviously spooked as most seven year olds would be. Being afraid of the dark anyway made it a particularly horrifying experience. I was even afraid to go to the bathroom sometimes, even urinating on myself from being frozen in fear. Those episodes made me love being outside all day just wishing daylight would last forever. Sadly, I begin to fear going to my own home.

I would yearn for a place to get away for a while, not complete separation but just a brief getaway. At this time in my life I would almost beg to spend the night at someone's house which was very rare. Just to get a break and experience a different environment. At that time the only stable adult that we were attached to was most often my uncle Charlie who invited Ronald and I to sleep over with our cousin Andre. I enjoyed these moments particularly because Uncle Charlie's wife, my aunt Faye was a traditional old school mother who prepared four course meals and even deserts before we went to bed. It was there were I got a taste of what would become my favorite desert, banana pudding.

I truly, envied my cousin Andre and his sister Nikkie. They had a fairly nice sized well-furnished home, not a crammed apartment. But what I envied most was the fact that they had both mother and father right there in their life every day. At that point, I had no idea who my real father was. Andre had his own room with lots of toys and fun things to do. I don't think they really appreciated how lucky they were. It was always difficult going back home after spending a couple of days in a nice stable environment. I use the word home generously; I don't believe my environment at times qualified as a home. A home is defined as a place where you belong. Nobody belongs in poverty or in a dangerous and unhealthy environment. I often wondered why I had to live in these stressful conditions of being poor, no father and a parent with a serious drinking problem. Some may argue that there is a lot worse a child could be forced to live in. From a global perspective we were a lot better off than starving kids in some third world countries such as Somalia or Ethiopia. However, the severity of an environment should be measured by the perception of the individual(s) affected. The challenge is that we sometimes do not clearly know the effects that environment has on a child until years later.

I had mixed emotions coming home after visiting someone. I would look forward to seeing my sober mother who would greet me with a warm hug and show some much needed affection. On the other hand my fear was of my alcoholic mother who would be too drunk to open the door when my uncle would drop us off.

I would be affected similarly when we would get rare visits from other family members. We enjoyed seeing family, particularly our cousins. The fact that there was those brief moments that we felt like we were not alone. We had family that cared and whom we could spend quality time with. Most of these visits though few were special because most family who visited knew my mother and knew what items not to bring, mainly, no wine, no beer, *no Joy Juice what so ever.* It was common knowledge that family members were never to bring any alcoholic beverages to any of our social gatherings. Spending time with people we haven't seen in a long while, receiving much needed attention from aunts and uncles, playing games, having a variety of food made these events very special.

The hardest part for me was when people would leave. I quite often would cry when it was time for family visitors to leave. When company was around she was usually sober and a very nice person. I did not want the fun to end nor did I want things to go back to normal which was not good for me. So whenever the time would come for folks to go home, I'd become sad and stand at the door crying, wishing they would stay longer or take me with them. Sometime, my sisters would take me to the back room to preoccupy me so our company could leave without feeling guilty by having to watch me cry like a baby as they left. I believe most people understood why I was sad to see them leave. They would always promise to comeback soon. The usual response was "We'll see ya again next weekend." particularly, my aunt who has four daughters around the same age as my sisters. She would always promise to come get me to spend the night at her house. It never happened. As I would stand at the door with tears rolling down my face, I can only imagine how sorry they felt for me as they drove home.

CHAPTER 12

TOUGH LOVE

"The brutal whipping I had suffered had a lasting effect on me. However, it didn't cure my vulnerability to peer pressure"

It was hard to determine whether it was the effects of the alcoholism or just old school tough love that we were being subjected to in the name of discipline. As a young severely underprivileged child, my desires for having things overwhelmed my self-control which lead me into a brief stage of dishonesty.

One afternoon I was asked by my mother who was entertaining a male guest, Mr. Johnson, to walk to the store to pick up a few items. Mr. Johnson, who was always a very generous individual, gave me several dollars to purchase a couple of necessities. It was a common courtesy that when you send a kid on such a long and dangerous journey to a store in south Central L. A., you reward him with some change which could be a quarter, 50 cent, even a whole dollar. A quarter is not much to ask considering all that could happen to a kid on the way to the store. In this particular neighborhood I was always on the lookout for one of the many loose dogs that could jump out and attack me at any given moment. There was also a neighborhood bully that loved jumping little guys and taking their money. If that wasn't enough, there were the ever present street gangs that had everyone on edge as they hovered at the corner of the block. After surviving all of that and walking several long blocks in cheap beat-up shoes "my shoes had so many holes in them, they looked like sandals", a young brother deserved a little treat for his efforts. So, I took the liberty of using a Dime of Mr. Johnsons change to get myself a pack of watermelon *Now & Laters* which was one of my favorite kind of candy at the time. I assumed that he wouldn't mind.

I had done this several times when my mother had sent me to the store with no wrath or consequences, however, this situation would produce a drastically different response. As I arrived with the grocery items still sucking on a piece of candy, my mother asked me in a calm voice, "Deon, where did you get the money to buy candy?" I almost froze for a moment as I instantly realized that I was in trouble. I slowly returned the rest of Mr. Johnson's change, still haven't responded to her question. She reemphasized, "Who told you to buy some candy with Mr. Johnson's money?" I sadly mumbled, "No body!" I could since that this awkward exchange was even making Mr. Johnson uncomfortable.

She ordered me to go directly to my room. At this time the other kids were outside and there was no one to brace me for what was about to happen. I was so nervous with fear I could not sit still. I paced back and forth in our room on the verge of having an anxiety attack. I even contemplated climbing out of the window and running away. Finally I considered that she wouldn't go off on me with company in the house would she? I thought at least she would wait until Mr. Johnson left to do whatever she was going to do to me. By that time one of my older brothers or sisters would be there to try to prevent her from doing something too crazy. I was wrong.

After a few minutes I could hear her angry feet pounding toward the room. I was already shedding tears of fear. She busted into the room with a fury whaling a thick electric extension cord. With every stroke that hit me it struck an excruciating streak of pain that felt like it was ripping off layers of my skin. My screams and pleads for her to stop had no effect. She showed no empathy as I cried out, "O.K.! I'm sorry, I won't do it again." She continued for what seemed like an hour, giving me a beating that no child ever deserves, particularly, an eight year old kid being beaten like a slave over a lousy dime. As the pounding and screaming continued I was hoping that Mr. Johnson who was a reasonable man would have some sympathy and come stop this nonsense. He never did. When she finally stopped hitting me probably from exhaustion, she was too tired to say anything but, "don't you ever do that again as long as you live."

Still whimpering from pain I could barely move. The extension cord left thick welts on my legs and back, some of which were bleeding. The wombs on my body were so painfully sensitive that I could not sit or lay on my back. I laid there in the prone position traumatized and clutching the mustard colored blanket that covered my twin bed. Mr. Johnson slowly walked into the room. There was nothing he could have said that could make me feel any better, but he tried. "Deon, you know I would have given you the money to buy candy. Why didn't you just ask me?" Obviously, I was not in any condition to explain, so he gently tapped me on the head and left the room. It was a sad revelation to me that even this well sized man could not protect me from my mother's wrath and instability.

What made her react with such a rage over something that seemed relatively minor? Why hadn't she reacted this way when I spent her money without asking? Was it because that what I did was embarrassing to her? As an adult, I realized that it was more likely a combination of exposing the act of being dishonest and stealing in the presence of company that angered her the most. We've all heard that saying, "don't act a fool in front of company." It must be o.k. to act a fool around family. It took me several days to physically heal from the whipping with the help of my sisters who nursed my wombs. My brothers were not very sympathetic. They had all gotten it like that before and thought that it was about time that I got a taste of a good butt whipping as if it was some sort of family initiation. Emotionally, the healing process took longer. I felt different towards my mother after that. Her rare hugs and affection was uncomfortable because I couldn't understand how someone who you know loves you can harm you in such a way.

As a parent as well as a professional in the field of youth-child development, my understanding of physical discipline has broadened. This has been an on-going debate that continues to cloud the African American family in terms of how we discipline our children. Some intellectuals theorized that these beatings are connected to the vicious whippings that were imposed upon our ancestors during the African Holocaust or slavery. The obvious flaw in that theory is that African Americans did not originate nor are they the only culture to use excessive corporal punishment on their children. Therefore what is the connection for other nationalities that also use leather straps or belts to discipline their children? This harsh brand of discipline has been a part of African American culture for generations. By today's standard my mother would have been arrested and charged with child abuse for imposing such harm to a child. However, in 1975 it was widely accepted as a normal and some people would argue necessary way of disciplining a child.

I support progressive discipline which means you gradually build up to higher or more aggressive tactics in order to correct a child's behavior pattern. Many parents don't have the patience to go through the progressive discipline process. They want an immediate impact that is often driven by anger and frustration. I've often heard my mother maintain that, "I had nine kids. When one of them did something seriously wrong, I'd whip their ass real good in front of the other kids to set an example for the others." I believe this tactic does have some roots from the slave trade. As African American historian and Author John Hope Franklin brought out in his book "From Slavery to Freedom", many slave owners use the same method to prevent or deter slaves from running away. They would hold these public beatings in the center of the plantation basically showcasing the punishment for a runaway.

The brutal whipping that I had suffered had a lasting effect on me. However, it didn't cure my vulnerability to peer pressure. My older brother Ronald had a way of manipulating me into doing some of the things that he was either too scared to do or needed me to join in on which is typical behavior between younger brothers. I was obviously naïve enough to fall for his schemes.

During a trip to the now notorious neighborhood Empire Market in South Central Los Angeles, we decided to fill our pockets with some walnuts that were on display in the produce section. Empire market is now known as the location where a young African American girl Latasha Harlins was shot and killed in 1991 for allegedly attempting to steal a carton of orange juice worth $1.97. The shooter was a female Korean store owner who was eventually given no jail time for the murder but community service. This is said to be one of the acts of injustices against African American people in the early 90s that sparked the Los Angeles riots in after the Rodney King verdict in 1992.

Nearly 20 years before, in the same store with a different name, to this day I have no idea why we decided to take walnuts. Taking the lead from Ronald, I stuffed several nice sized walnuts in my pockets. I must have looked ridiculous because my pockets were so packed I could hardly walk.

As we casually passed through the exit doors we were approached by a casually dressed Caucasian gentleman. He politely asked us to follow him back into the store. When we hesitated he briefly showed us a badge that he removed from his rear pocket. We instantly realized that we were busted. Before we even made it to the security room upstairs, my eyes were glazed and tears rolled down my cheek. I'm not sure what Ronald was thinking but I was more afraid of the rage of my mother more so than the consequences of the local authorities. As the security guy and the store manager begin to explain the situation to us, we begin to plead for forgiveness. They finally came to the conclusion by stating, "Were not going to call the police this time, but if I catch you stealing in my store again you're going to be arrested".

The poor man had no idea that we could care less about being arrested we just didn't want our mother to hear about this. Unfortunately, as we thought we were getting off easy, he uttered the words that we feared the most . . ." Now what is your home phone number so we can have your parents come down to here to get you." Ronald generated enough nerve to ask if we could just go without him calling our mother. He responded, "It's either your parents or the police. Now what's it going to be boys?" My choice was obvious but Ronald gave in to the fact that either way she was going to be involved so he reluctantly gave the gentleman our next door neighbors number. We had no home phone at the time. Whoever answered would go next door to deliver the message to my mother.

As we anxiously waited, concerned of my mother response, I was thinking of ways to explain my action to lessen the anticipated punishment. By the time she arrived at the store I was a bundle of nerves as I feared what the next few hours would bring. She was unusually polite to the store manager which meant that she was saving her wrath for us. As we begin what seemed like a 100 mile long walk home, her initial reaction puzzled me. It seemed that she was not as agitated at the fact that we had stolen something but she appeared to be more upset at what we stole. Her actual reaction was, "of all the shit in the store yawl gonna try to steal some damn nuts? If you're gonna steal, at least steal something that we can use."

To my surprise we got no whipping which also puzzled me. I knew she would do something but I didn't know what, until dinner time. Ronald and I were perplexed as to what was going to be the punishment up until that point. She was acting as though nothing happened at all. She prepared a nice little meal and was not intoxicated at all. As we sat down for dinner my sisters seem to have the edge of knowledge over us because they were aware of what was about to go down. Just after she place a full plate of food on the table for my sisters, she paused a moment. She looked at Ronald and I and said, "oh, since you guys like walnuts so much that you need to steal. Here is your dinner." She placed a huge fruit bowl full of walnuts in front of us. ". . . and you damn well better finish every last one of them." We were force to eat walnuts all week long for breakfast, lunch and dinner. After a few days I was physically sick. Understandably my taste and tolerance for walnuts is zero. To this day I can't stand the smell or taste of walnuts. It was a lesson learned.

From that point on I begin to seriously consider the consequences of my actions. Actually, it was the fear of those consequences that prevented reckless thoughtless actions. Was it the harsh or creative discipline that steered my development into a responsible adult? I believe there are multitudes of experiences coupled with hereditary traits and influences that plays a significant role in the development of a man.

According to some psycho therapist, there are personality traits, facial features and talents that are passed on genetically from parents to their offspring. Some even believe that negative traits are passed on as well, such as susceptibility to alcoholism and drug addiction. I believe in the strange truth that even criminal behavior could possibly be hereditary. From a divine perspective, it is written that we are all imperfect by inheriting sin from our original parents Adam and Eve. My family experience gives more credence to this.

I have family members who have had no relations or physical influence with their biological father since early childhood. All through their preteens, adolescents and early adulthood, these two family members in particular seem to suffer from the very same illness that caused their biological father to spend most of his adult life in prison. He was a kleptomaniac. This cat was a gifted thief. He could steal the watch off of your wrist without you even knowing it. As long as I have known him, I don't believe he ever paid for anything that he had, other than food. No one on the mother's side of the family had this issue. There was no significant time spent with the father to have influenced the children. So, one has to wonder.

As a mentor of young people, one of my first projects for the youth that I work with is to research their family history and bloodline. Most of the time this results in positive revelations such as learning about significant family accomplishments and success stories. There are also those necessary but not so proud discoveries that should move us to become conscious and proactive to break the cycle of negative or ill spirited traits that could affect the quality of a person's life.

Chapter 13

Nine Months

"At home we hardly ever had brand named cereal not even corn flakes. We always had the generic version called Flakes Corn."

The true identity of my biological father has been a family mystery for years until I was nine years old. During one of my mother's drinking parties, which seem like a major neighborhood event, she casually called my attention to a strange man in the crowd of familiar faces. He was a rugged looking man with brown skin and a receding hairline. "That's your Daddy." she said in a calm voice. I was shocked and visibly disappointed. Ronald and I would often compare exaggerated stories about what our fathers who we knew nothing about had or would do for us someday. By this time, we did know that we had different fathers, which fueled the flames of comparing whose daddy had the best car, the most money or was in the best physical shape. Well, by the looks of this guy, I had lost that argument in every category. He looked like Woody the wino. I actually thought it was some kind of joke. As kids growing up in the 70s, we would regularly tease each other with playful harmless wisecracks about each other's Daddy. Mainly because most of us never really knew our real fathers, so it was never delivered or received as a personal insult. However, if you were to talk about someone's mamma you might just get your lip busted.

I had a serious case of self-deception because I actually pictured my father as a tall, classy, well dressed businessman. This person looked homeless. I was experiencing a real life, "Yo daddy . . ." joke. There was plenty of times that I would be walking with one of my friends and see a bum lying in the alley, when someone would say . . . "That's your Daddy!" I never thought they could be right. This man looked like he was living a rough life. He had on a pair of dirty overalls. It was actually a jumpsuit uniform which I assumed he at least had a job. As my mother formally introduced us, we shared an awkward hand shake and a hug. After a brief embrace, I noticed a strong scent of cologne with an even stronger scent of body odor which made this first impression even more uncomfortable. Who in their right mind would be wearing cologne over a dirty musty jumpsuit? That's sort of like sprinkling potpourri over a pile of dog mess. I also noticed that his hands were dark from what looked like oil stains. The insides of his hands were darker than the outside, which is something that I had never seen before.

He introduced himself as Larry. The name sounded familiar as I quickly recall my sisters teasing me about my daddy named Larry. As we sat down in the living room the party crowd was now reduced to the immediate family and a few others. Still a bit uncomfortable with his presence, I sat extremely close to my mother as they spoke about me possibly spending time with him. Pretending not to be paying attention to what they were saying, I quickly turned my attention toward them when I heard him say, "you had nine years, now give me nine years." At the time, I was perplexed yet not as annoyed as I was later at his ridiculous request. To my knowledge, this guy had never spent a significant minute with me in my entire life. How dare he show up after nine years and have the audacity to ask such a thing, as if he had earned any parental points.

My older Brother Herman often asked the reasonable question . . ." where in the hell was he when we were going in and out of those foster homes?" This was a fair question for all of our relatively close family members including our fathers, uncles, aunts and grandfather. Herman would occasionally remind us to ask ourselves this question when one of our *fair weather* relatives would come out of the blue with some phony expressions of love and concern for us. Had my mother not been in an altered state of mind, she may have told him to . . . *"Go to hell with gasoline drawers."* which would not have surprised anyone. Instead she looked at me and simply asked me, "do you want to go live with him?"

What an awkward situation to put a nine year old boy in. The man is sitting here staring me right in the face. How could I say no? Outside of his immediate presence, my response would've been, not just no, but Hell no which would have probably earned me a slap in the lips from the

lightning quick hands of my mom. Although he was
a perfect stranger, I begin to consider my current
living environment and begin to think. What did
I have to lose? There was the remote possibility that
pops here, despite his Black Bozo like appearance,
could provide a rich and comfortable environment.
So my options were simple. Either I stay here in
an overcrowded apartment in the ghetto of South
Central Los Angeles with an alcoholic mother who
could barely provide for us, or take what's behind
door number 3. After further review of the situation,
I learned that my father was actually a pretty stable
individual. He was a mechanic which explained
his appearance when I first met him. He was also
a truck driver who owned several big rigs which
required him to travel throughout the U.S. quite
regularly.

That night they simply made the reasonable
decision to just let me spend time with him over
the weekend and take it from there. After packing
a small overnight bag, I waved to my siblings and
gave my mom a hug as we left. I did feel somewhat
special because at that time neither of my brothers or
sisters had seen or heard from their fathers in at least
a year. We drove away in a small blue truck. I was

excited just to be going somewhere. This was also the first time I had been allowed to sit in the front seat of a car. I could barely see over the hood. He noticed me struggling to see, so he pulled out a pillow from behind the seat for me to sit on.

The vehicle reeked of gasoline but I didn't mind at all. We drove for about 30 minutes through the dark L.A. streets during which he asked me several questions like, what is my favorite subject in school and do I play any sports? It was just enough small talk to make up for nine years of abandonment. Our first stop was not to his home but some type of mechanics shop. I sat in the car as he went inside for what seemed like 12 years. I had to use the bathroom really bad but didn't have the nerve or the sense to just get out of the car and ask if I could go. Instead, I held it, hoping he would come out soon. My legs were waging side to side while my bladder felt like it was going to explode any second. By this time, I was in tears as I started to wet myself. Finally, I see him walking toward the car. He immediately recognized my uncomfortable expression and asked me what was wrong? "I gotta pee." I mumbled. He opened the car door and I dashed inside the building.

It was safe to say that the jury was still out on whether I liked Mr. Larry or not. I didn't even know what to call him. It was too soon for me to call him Daddy or anything associated with fatherhood. As we continued our night drive, he lectured me on speaking up for myself when I wanted or needed something. At this time, I was still a reserved and withdrawn kid who sometimes had trouble communicating with close relatives, let alone strangers. I was still extremely uncomfortable around him and my first impression of him so far had not made it any easier. This is the first time we've seen each other in at least nine years and the first thing he does is leave me in a stinky, smelly truck at night for 45 minutes. What a dad!

We finally arrived at a nice residence on an unfamiliar part of Los Angeles. It was a well groomed duplex in a quiet looking neighborhood. It was now nearly midnight. As we parked the vehicle and entered the residence, he instructed me to sit in the living room until he returned from the bedroom. I overheard him speaking to a woman who I assumed was his wife or girlfriend. At this point, I was thoroughly confused and didn't know what to think. From what I observed just sitting there in the well decorate, slightly dark living room, was that this place was extremely neat and well taken care of. It seemed to be uncharacteristic of my newly discovered father who showed me no signs of being a neat squeaky clean person.

After a brief moment, he returned to the living room with a blanked and pillow. Closely behind him was a very nice looking, younger woman who introduced herself as Ruby. Although she was in her sleeping attire, I could tell that she was a very attractive lady. This woman and my father appeared to be an obvious mismatch. After helping me settle in on the sofa, they returned to their room. The bedding and sofa was quite warm and very comfortable yet I could not sleep. I began to feel that uncomfortable feeling of being in an unfamiliar place. I recalled that same type of feeling during my experiences in foster homes. That slightly insecure feeling usually stayed with me for months.

Although the house was quiet with a fresh flowery scent, the stench of betrayal would quickly taint the environment. As I lay there unable to sleep, I could still clearly hear their conversation in the other room. "Larry! Who is that little boy?" She asked.

He paused a moment then responded, "I'm not sure! I actually found him on the street by himself. I couldn't leave the kid out there like that. We'll deal with it in the morning." I couldn't believe what I was hearing. I immediately sat up feeling both angry and ashamed. This guy darn near begs my mother to let me spend time with him then brings me here and lie about who I am. Was he ashamed to tell her that I was his son? Why would he tell her that he found me in the street? I'm not homeless. Just when I was beginning to feel loved and cared for, those words made me feel more worthless than ever before. I wanted to get the heck out of there. I stood up, threw off the cover and stepped toward the door. As I diligently tried to open the door without making any noise, reality kicked in when I realized that it was after 1am and I had no idea where the hell I was. I had no money and couldn't call because we had no telephone at home. If I walked out that door, I really would be a lost homeless boy. So, I humbly swallowed my pride, laid my mad behind right back down and silently cried myself to sleep.

The next morning, I woke up to a different voice. "Ah, hello". It was a young girl about my age. "Who are you?" she asked nicely. "My name is Deon" I replied wiping my eyes as I struggle to focus. "Well, Good Morning" she continued. "What kind of cereal would you like?" I thought, wow, you mean I get a choice. Not wanting to sound impressed I responded, "It doesn't matter."

As we walked toward the kitchen, my father approached us and introduced the young girl as Pam. "Pam, this is your brother Deon, he lives with his mother on the other side of town." Not realizing that she was behind him, Ms. Ruby startled him as she firmly asked him, "Larry, why did you lie to me last night?" she continued now standing directly in front of him. "You could have told me the truth. Why didn't you tell me you had a son?" She quickly defused the mild stand off as she apparently realized that it was making me feel a bit uneasy. Looking at me with concern, she wisely suggested that they continue this conversation later and proceeded to help Pam prepare breakfast.

She was actually very hospitable considering the circumstances, again asking me what kind of cereal did I like. As she opened the cupboard my eyes grow wide with excitement as I saw several boxes of my favorite types of cereal. There was Captain

Crunch, Trix, Fruit loops and more. It was an underprivileged kids dream. At home, we hardly ever had brand named cereal, not even corn flakes. We always had the generic version called Flakes Corn that would get soggy even before you put milk in it.

This situation was evident of how adult confrontations could damage the emotional wellbeing of a child. This argument could have quickly escalated into a loud and ugly scene which would have negatively affected me as well as their daughter Pam. Although, by that time, I was already damaged goods. The way Ms. Ruby handled this situation was considerate. Although she had every right to confront my father for his thoughtless actions that put each one of us in an awkward situation, she set aside her own emotions for the wellbeing of the children which is what responsible adults should do.

I was hoping that my feelings toward my father and this new environment would soon grow into a place of love and comfort. Considering my first 12 hours with him, it didn't give me much confidence in his sincerity or his parenting skills.

I was hopeful that my father's passionate request for my mother to give him nine years with me meant that he was eager to be that proud loving supportive dad that every child needs. Unfortunately, he never became that person. Naturally, it took me a while to feel comfortable around this new family. I spent the weekend with them and returned home. I never told my mother about my first experience with my father. I knew that if I mentioned that he had left me in his truck inhaling gasoline fumes for nearly an hour, then told his girlfriend that he had found me on the streets, I would have never seen him again. After my second visit, I was much more at ease being around my new sister and Ms. Ruby. It was agreed that I would stay with them over the summer. As a big rig truck driver, my father was away most of the time. Over that time, I began to establish a bond with my new sister Pam and Ms. Ruby. They treated me very well as though I was always a part of their family. We went places and experienced things that I never have before. As a child in a small family, I begin to receive the individual attention that often eluded children in large families. Obviously, you can certainly do more things financially with two kids as appose to nine.

I recognized and appreciated that reality the first time we went grocery shopping together. The first pleasant surprise that I noticed was that Ms. Ruby actually allowed us to participate in the selection of the food. What a culture shock it was to have the choice of picking out my very own box of cereal. I couldn't believe it! I was so excited I wanted to start doing cart wheels down the Aisles. Pam chose Sugar Smacks and I went straight for the Crunch Berries. There are simple moments like these that bring so much joy to the hearts of children that some adults sadly over look. As a parent, what is a couple of extra dollars to you when it could generate such pleasure for a child?

With my new second family, I also experienced my first visit to an amusement park. At home, the closest we got to an amusement park is when my mother would let us jump on the bed. She would sometimes tell us that we were going by Disneyland. We would get all excited but she never said we were going in. We would just drive by just like she said we would. One could understand how excited I was to learn that we were going to Six Flags Magic Mountain. They invited a few other kids, family and friends none of which I knew. My Dad, Ms. Ruby and other adults made a camp style picnic in the grass area near the front of the park while the kids went for the joy rides.

Being that this was my first experience at a huge amusement park, I was a bit overwhelmed. It was the weekend of the Fourth of July holiday so it was extremely crowded with people. Before long I got lost in the crowd and spent the majority of the day alone looking for my sister and the rest of the kids. I didn't know my way around, so I was literally walking around completely lost. Throughout the entire day I managed to get on only two rides. By the time I did find at least the way back to the picnic area where the adults were, it was dark and I was tired and hungry. It turned out to be a miserable first experience at Six Flags Magic Mountain. It would be years before I would return to the theme park.

After the summer my father insisted on me staying with them in order to place me in a better school. That fall I was placed in the same catholic school as my new sister Pam. It was a drastic change from the public school that I was attending with my mother. Although it was a bit uncomfortable for me, I did feel special and cared for. The whole private school environment was something that we were always on the opposite side of. While we often teased them for the corny uniforms that they wore, we actually envied them at the same time for their upper middle class status.

Many people had lost faith in the public school system in the Los Angeles Unified School District at the time. They believed that the LAUSD was not worthy enough for their children yet they could not afford the alternative which was private school. Were the public schools so bad, that you had to pay several thousand dollars a semester for your children to learn Basic English, Math and Science?

Sending your child to a public school these days could be as dangerous and uncomfortable as sending them to California Youth Authority. With constant budget cuts, an unruly population, overcrowded classrooms and a burned-out, overworked staff, the environment and atmosphere on school campuses is often precarious or discouraging.

Most secondary school campuses are as socially and racially divided as prison yards. The athletes, the gamers, the skaters, the cheerleaders, the geeks, the hustlers and the gangsters are all congregated in their own groups. No matter how often I encourage students to diversify their social network (and I often have to emphasis that that has nothing to do with Facebook or Twitter) it just doesn't manifest on school campus.

Most parents that I have spoken with in recent years who have not giving up and evacuated the public school system for charter or private schools, have remained by circumstances only, not by choice. Although I am also a concerned parent, I have not yet abandoned the concept of an enriching public educational institution. My Catholic school experience with my second family actually made me appreciate public school.

My first Christmas with my second family gave me a snapshot of the life of a privileged child. It was the first time that I experience having a real pine tree. We went to a lot that was selling nearly hundreds of trees. It was a joyful experience not only selecting a huge tree but finding lights and decorations for it. There were so many wrapped presents that they were stacked up as high as half of the height of the tree.

Christmas with my original family was far from jolly. We had a tree that was given away to those who lived in the Watts housing projects. It was an aluminum tree with tree branches you had to screw in. Each year, we would lose several branches. By the time I was 9 years old, we only had about two or three branches left. It was a pitiful site and worse than Charlie Brown's Christmas tree.

After the first semester, I would return to my mother's home at her request. I would later learn that my father was actually married to another woman at the time of my conception and while he was involved with Ms. Ruby, so both my sister Pam and I were born out of wedlock. This also explained why he was gone most of the time that I spent with Ms. Ruby and Pam. He was doing double time between his wife and a second family. My very existence was intentionally kept as a secret from his original family. It would be over thirty years until my father and I would ever speak again.

His absence would have a tremendous effect on the quality of my life. As a father of four, I honor that role as the most paramount position a man could hold. This raises a profound question to a father.

What are you doing to secure a quality future for your offspring? Have you established a trust fund that will grow interest over the years? You could leave them a fortune which could be blown in a short period of time if they are not trained to be financially responsible. Is it wise to simply provide for their needs but not provide them with the tools necessary to eventually provide for themselves? I like the biblical-related illustration that says, 'don't just feed your son, teach him to fish . . .' If you just feed him, he will eat for a day. If you teach him to fish, he will provide for himself and his family for a life time.

One of the best investments is to give them your most valuable possession which is you. Don't just spend money, spend time. Don't just tell them what is right or wrong, show them by providing a solid foundation of good morals and ethics. A friend of mine shared with me how the fine examples you show your child is like a bank deposit you make that will earn interest over time. You may not witness the benefits until years later. I often question my own integrity as a father. Am I spending too much time outside the home? Am I being too ambitious with career objectives? Have I invested the same amount of time and energy with each of my children? We are often overzealous with our first child and not as enthusiastic with your last. If you have 8 million pictures of your first child and only three of your last, there's a problem. The last child often gets the raw deal. As the last of nine, I am living proof. To this day, I can't find a single picture of me as a baby. I'm not sure if I was adopted, abducted, born or hatched.

A highly effective father will establish a healthy balance in how he prioritizes his time. There are some men who believe that as long as they are providing financial support, they are doing enough and are meeting their parental obligations. Without providing quality time, proper guidance, influence, affection, discipline and emotional support, you are falling short of your responsibility as a father.

CHAPTER 14

SOUTH PARK—EAST L.A.

"... you have to leave a room to inhale a different air to realize that the room you were in, actually stinks."

In the summer of 1978 we were on the move again. This time it was to 51st and Avalon in South East Los Angeles. Once again, it was not a voluntary relocation. We were in a situation where we were being evicted quite frequently and this move was no different. The resident was a small one bedroom green and white duplex with a large park directly across the street. I'm sure this was a big selling point for the landlords trying to rent this place. Of course they would hope that the would be tenants were too ignorant to have picked up a local newspaper in the last two years to discover the fact that this beautiful park is also one of the most gang and drug infested locations in all of L.A. I was too young to understand and my mother was probably too detached to realize what we were moving into. We were on welfare so our financial circumstances probably did not give us the luxury of choice. I'm sure a beach front apartment in Malibu was not an option.

My first impression of the place when we first visited it was very pleasant. It was a bright sunny yet dangerously smoggy afternoon as usual. There were some days when a deep breath would send a powerful and painful streak of bad air that would literally choke me. We were to meet the landlord to view the property and sign a lease. Mr. Landlord was about an hour late so we spent the time waiting across the street at South Park, just in time for the free lunch that was provided every week day in the summer. As I enjoy the roast beef sandwich and chocolate milk, I'm thinking, wow, a huge park with free lunch, we *have* to move here.

The park was fairly large in size with one side beautifully lined with large oak trees and a huge grassy area. The other side had the recreation office, basketball courts a baseball diamond and a swimming pool. There were houses that completely surrounded the park. Our new place was a duplex directly across the street.

After the meeting, I was pleased when my mother informed me that we would be moving in next week. The only down side was that this was just a one bed room which meant that obviously there wasn't enough room for all of us. Two of my sisters were staying with older siblings so it was just me Ronald and Mommy moving in.

We moved-in several days later with the help of my oldest brother Herman who was now married with a small family of his own. He was always there when things got rough for us or when we needed something, even discipline. We didn't have much by way of furniture, we had just a few things and lots of boxes. The first night was a bit uncomfortable because we had no lights. The electricity would not be shut on until the next day, so we just sat on the floor and talked. I was excited about going to the park the next day and maybe meeting some friends. Ronald complained about being hungry so my mother and I decided to walk to the nearest store.

We knew there would be an open liquor store or something nearby. At the time, we didn't realize how dangerous and foolish it was to be out at this time in this neighborhood. We walked a good seven or eight blocks until we found a store that was open this time of night. I was hoping she would not buy alcoholic beverages so I was a bit nervous as we walked into Wendell's Liquor store on 58th and Avalon.

We purchased a small box of Rice Crispy cereal, a half a gallon of milk, a can of Sardines and some crackers. It was far from the A list of groceries but at 3am in a neighborhood liquor store, what would you expect. I was just happy that the usual half a pint of vodka wasn't on the list. The walk home was much more pleasant because I was eating a pack of watermelon Now & Laters. The next morning we realize that we forgot to purchase sugar for the cereal. Eating Rice Crispys with no sugar is a dreadful experience.

The first day was exciting as I got up to cross the street to explore the new surroundings. Ronald and I started from the front side of the park taking in all of the elements and smells. We analyzed every wino, every bum, every man woman or child that we saw in or around the park that day. As we walked through a small tunnel that led to the swimming pool and sports area, we were excited about the potential for fun. It was the middle of the summer so the swimming pool was already busy. The fresh and potent familiar aroma of chlorine that filled the air signified the summer atmosphere in L.A. My eyes lit up as I saw a small candy store near the recreation office which was in the center of the park.

Just pass the office where you could check out balls and equipment, were two huge basketball courts. The first time I saw this court it had an effect on me that I could not understand at the time. The sun was bright and appeared to be centered exactly on the courts like a spot light and all eyes were on the players. There was music blasting from a large radio or ghetto blaster playing what would become the inarguable anthem for hip hop culture, "Rapper's Delight". Ronald and I just stood there admiring the scene for a while in a sort of daze. I was instantly in love with this environment. There were adults, teens and younger kids all engaged in different games of competitive play. I could not wait to get involved. Beyond the hoop court which was the center of attention at the park was another 100 yards of green grass and a baseball diamond. This was an awesome scene on the surface but we had no idea that we were also in grave danger.

We never really realized how dangerous this neighborhood was at the time. It is difficult to get a proper view of a situation from such a close perspective. Sometimes you have to take a step back to get a clear outlook of an environment. Another example is how you have to leave a room to inhale a different air to realize that the room you were in actually stinks.

CHAPTER 15

THE IMPACT OF HOOP SKILLS

"I wore a cheap brand of black and white sneakers called Pro-Keds which had two stripes. I would use a black marker to draw another stripe to make them look like Adidas . . ."

I believe that the closest that I have ever come to an epiphany, was when I begin playing basketball at South Park. I had been playing ball occasionally in school for about a year. Therefore, I was not completely new to the game but it all came together at the park. Maybe it was the environment, the energy from the sun or maybe a combination of the two. It was also a special time for the sport of basketball which was growing in popularity. The late 70s is now referred to as the golden years of the NBA with stars like Dr. J and George "The Ice

Man" Gervin. However, it was the phenomenal arrival of Larry Bird and Magic Johnson that sent NBA excitement to unprecedented heights.

I was 11 years old when I first witnessed the joy of seeing Magic Johnson play. It was the 1979 NCAA national championship verses Indiana State and Larry Bird. It may have been the first time that I felt completely engaged by a basketball game. I watched his every move which was quite a challenge because we only had a tiny black and white half broken T.V. with a dying picture tube. There was a thick black line that ran through the screen that made it hard to follow the action. Ronald and I were both hooked from that point on, on the game and the player as Magic showed off his playmaking skills to win the National championship for Michigan State. Just a few months later he would be coming to L.A. as the first draft pick for the Los Angeles Lakers.

It was a very exciting time to be in Los Angeles if you were a basketball fan. We watched Magic and the Lakers games every time they aired on KTVU Channel 13. After every game I would head to the park the next day to try to imitate him on the black top. The Lakers showtime style of play featuring Magic, definitely fueled my addiction to the game. As I became a better player, I begin to earn respect from kids who were my age and older which was something that I truly needed at the time. Prior to that, I had very low self-esteem and no self-confidence. Due to our family instability, I was always the new kid in school or in the hood. I was also self-conscious because I was always one of the smallest kids and not very well dressed. I wore obvious hand me down clothes and worn-out gym shoes that were purchased at the local super market. The brand of shoe was Pro-Keds which was a white shoe with two black stripes. I would find a black marker and draw a third stripe so they would look like Adidas.

However, on the basketball court, I was the man. I was short but quick which made me feel large and in charge. My confidence was incredible. I felt like I could beat anyone my age who stepped on the court and I usually did. I begin to develop a bit of a swagger that carried into my normal social life. I was changing from this shy reserved kid with very low self-esteem to a confident and at times almost arrogant personality.

As an adult, my experience in youth development moves me to encourage parents to explore a variety of activities for their child. I am living proof that when a child finds that activity that brings them a since of accomplishment, their self-esteem is improved dramatically. The modern term that today's culture uses is *swagger*. My increased confidence or swagger, even effected my off court personality. My since of humor became more of a defense tactic that I used to attack or embarrass anyone who dared to tease me for my worn out shoes or out dated clothes.

As a curious eleven year old, basketball was my only outlet from an un-nurturing and sometimes hazardous home environment. There was now a place where I could go to get away from the depressing condition in which I lived. After or most of the time instead of homework, I would grab a snack and jog across the street to the park to play ball. I'd meet the same group of kids every day at the park. Most of them were from the same elementary school. Some were older and others was just kids from the neighborhood. We had a special competitive camaraderie that was sort of addictive. The drama and challenge of winning or losing with a group of friends made it fun but serious. There were times we would argue and even come to blows over a game but at the end of the day we would look forward to doing it again the next day. It became an environment similar to an exclusive country club. Your acceptance depended on how well you could play. If you had hoop skills you were in.

Being accepted in a social environment is extremely critical for older children and teens. A strong and stable family relationship usually will supplement for the lack of social acceptance. Unfortunately, it is often times a negative influence that replaces the family relationship such as gangs, street hustling, drug activities or criminal mischief. In this particular section of Los Angeles, it was either drug dealing or drug using that occupied the time of most youth.

Those who managed to abstain from the ills of drugs and gangs were some sort of athlete. This is the sad illusion that existed and still exists in the African American community. It tells a young man that the only way he can elevate himself from the conditions of the hood is to be an athlete, an entertainer or a drug dealer. That message would continue to be reemphasized through media, film, music and peers.

My gravitation toward the game of basketball was a positive diversion. Soon the game of basketball transcended all personal responsibilities.

When I was engaged in a game, I didn't have a care or concern that would alter my focus. My only concern was how I was going to score on the guy defending me which was more of a problem for him than me. My issues with my mother or not having clothes that fit were not a factor at all while I was playing ball.

However, as in most cases the conditions in one aspect of your life eventually does affect the other. I was at the park *going to work* on these kids in a game of three on three. I'm doing my thing scoring passing and making plays that put my team up for game point which means the next point and we win. It's every ball player's goal to hit the game winning bucket. So, not only was I intending to take the last shot but I was going to make it look good. I had the ball at the top of the key showcasing my ball handling skills when I noticed all of the other players looking at me laughing. I didn't think much of it until my own teammates and the guy guarding me begin to back up and join them in laughter. "What?" I yelled. They all pointed at my feet at the same time. I looked down and noticed that my sock was hanging through the bottom of my right shoe from a hole. It was flapping through like a second tongue. I was so embarrassed I just dropped the ball and ran home.

That was the first time that my home life had effected the comfort zone of my socio-athletic environment. Until that moment it was the only place where I felt respected by my peers. I didn't have that feeling of respect at home, at school or any other place. Now the one place where I had built a decent reputation seems to be ruined. As I ran home both angry and upset, angry at the kids who laughed at me and upset because there was nothing I could do about it. It was the only pair of shoes I had which I had worn out for almost a year. I was also upset because I knew I could not go back to the park with these raggedy shoes and I had no idea when or if I would get another pair.

I had gotten to the point that I didn't even ask my mother for money anymore. I knew it was one time only when she could afford to get us anything and that was at the beginning of school in September. It was now November so my only hope to get something was if someone would be nice enough to get me something for Christmas or my birthday in January which was almost two months away. There is no way I can go that long without playing ball.

When I made it home, I told my older brother Ronald what happened at the park. He looked at my shoes and laughed the same way those kids did across the street. After about 10 minutes of enjoyment at my expense, he finally recognized my pain and offered a suggestion. "Why don't you call Herman and see if he could hook you up?" It was a good idea but I had never asked anybody for anything besides candy. My older brother Herman always looked out for us when it came to clothes and food when we were in need. We could always count on him and his wife Jackie to provide at least one or two things to open on Christmas and birthdays. So I had convinced myself that this was a legitimate request. My angle was to tell him that I had no shoes to wear to school which was true but my main concern was getting back out there on the basketball court.

We still had no telephone at home, so I found a dime in the sofa and walked down to the corner store to use the pay phone. Normally, I would have just walked next door to Ms. Brown's house to ask to use her phone but this was a bit personal and people were nosey as hell around these parts. I rehearsed what I was going to say as I walked to the pay phone. It's a lot easier asking your parent for something like this because it is their responsibility. But to have to call someone at night out of the blue and ask them something like this was really hard to do for an eleven year old. I was pretty nervous and my heart was pounding as I dialed the number. As soon as he heard my voice he responded, "what's wrong?" It was a reasonable question because we would usually call him when something was wrong. The only difference was that it was never my voice on the other side of those calls so he sounded even more anxious than normal when he asked, "Boy where are you?" I answered, "I'm up the street at a pay phone. I was calling to see if you could get me some new shoes." He sounded a bit more relaxed when he asked, "what happen to the shoes you had?" "They got a big hole in the bottom of them." I said.

He quickly ended the conversation and told me to . . . "Get off that corner and go home". I felt a pleasant relief as I walked home. He instructed Ronald and me to take the bus tomorrow after school up to his job to purchase some new tennis shoes. He worked at a sporting goods store called, "Western Surplus".

The next day I was so excited about going to get some new kicks that I literally ran home from school. Ronald and I took the RTD—Rapid Transit District bus ride down Vermont Street to my brothers' job who worked as a sales associate. He introduced us to his coworkers as if he was a proud father instead of an older brother. He introduced me as the baby of the family and how I was a smart kid who wants to be a writer. Even though he had no idea about my new obsession for the game of basketball and that writing was the last thing on my mind, his words at that moment made me feel special. It was rare that anyone spoke of us in that regard as if they were really proud of us. That moment inspired me to want to do well in school because now I actually had someone who would appreciate my accomplishments.

At that time my mother was too far consumed by alcoholism that she paid very little attention to what was going on with us academically or socially. I don't recall her making a fuss about grades or school work during that time. However, Ronald and I had to have a good answer when Herman asked us about our grades or school work. Although, we would lie and say we were doing good even if we were failing. There was no sophisticated computer generated reports that were sent home at the time. You could easily turn an F into a B by the time you arrived home. I receive a slightly shocking reality gesture from my mother that revealed her alcoholic induced disinterest in my education. This particular Monday morning wore on me to the point that I just did not want to get moving to school. I was not feeling well but it certainly was not an illness or medical issue. I simply didn't feel like going to school.

After a couple of firm requests for me to get my "Narrow ass up" and get ready for school, I reluctantly, responded. "I'm not going to school today". Her response was both alarming and revealing, "Oh, I don't care where you go. But you're gettn the hell out of here." She made it quite clear to me that she couldn't care less about my education. She just wanted me out of the house."

Meanwhile at the Western Surplus, Herman took us around the store picking out shoes and trying on clothes. I'm not sure how much of a discount he received on purchasing items there but we left there with several bags filled with clothes and a fresh pair of leather converse. This was my first pair of real leather athletic shoes. The clothes were nice and very much appreciated but the prize for me was the Converse. It took every ounce of discipline for me not to strap them on and wear them right out of the store. I could not wait to get out on the court at South Park to break them in. While most of the other kids were still wearing the flimsy canvas Chuck Taylor's. I would be one of the few to hit the black top with the new White and Black trimmed leather converse all-stars.

This was not the first time my oldest brother had to bail me out of a crisis. He is also responsible for me experiencing my sixth grade graduation. I had accepted the fact that I was not going to attend my own graduation from elementary school for the simple fact that I had nothing even close to a reasonable outfit to wear. I owned nothing but hand me downs and athletic clothes. So that morning, I had sat there extremely disappointed, wanting to go but not wanting to embarrass myself by showing up looking like a "Down town L.A. Bum." To my surprise, I see my brother Herman drive up and step out the car with a plush brand new blue suit with a matching tie and a powder blue shirt. I met him at the door and before I could even get a word out, he urged me to, "Get dressed blood so we're not late." He handed me the suit. My mother smiled as if she knew this was going to happen all along.

Putting on a fresh new three piece suit for the first time is a moment that I will always remember. I even had a matching handkerchief and patent leather black shoes. I was one of the sharpest dudes on stage that day as I walked across the platform to receive my diploma with a "George Jefferson" swagger.

As we left the Surplus Store in a very pleasant mood and returned home from the 20 minute bus ride, we noticed several police and emergency vehicles at the park. We knew something really bad had happened because we saw a police helicopter hovering over the park lighting up the night. The Ghetto Bird which is what we called the police helicopter would shine a light so bright that it would look like broad daylight. As we eagerly approached, we learned that someone had been shot and killed near the back of the park. It was an eerie feeling to see a body covered with a yellow tarp which meant someone was dead at the scene. It was a somber ending to an otherwise great day for me.

The incident made the evening news. By this time South Park had a notoriously poor reputation and this latest murder obviously made the situation worse. The next time we spoke, our brother Herman demanded that we stay away from that park. It was a bit unreasonable to think it would be easy to keep two athletic boys from going to a park that was right across the street from home. I didn't care about what other people thought about South Park. To me it was the place to be, all day every day. Was my exposure to violence somehow causing me to be callas or insensitive to violence? Not really! I was just so hooked on playing basketball that it wouldn't have mattered if we were in the middle of the Vietnam

War during the late 60s, I was still going to be out there playing ball. So regardless of *Sergeant* Herman's order, we were right back across the street the next day. I had some much needed damage control to my reputation that I needed to take care of.

The game of basketball provided the protective shield that prevented us from gravitating toward criminal activity, addiction and insanity that eluded the majority of my older sisters. My brother Ronald was also an outstanding ball player who had a reputation of being a clutch shooter and a "*hot dog*" on the court. Like many urban athletes, basketball would be the vehicle that would take him from the streets of L.A. to a college education at Fresno State University. Trying to keep up with him fueled my competitive spirit which still benefits me to this day. He introduced me to the game and inspired me to get better. Basketball also provided me with much a needed social-athletic identity at a very critical time in my life. So many young people in similar situations tend to fall prey to negative influences due their vulnerability and unstable family life.

Although South Park was a far cry from a healthy environment for a child, it was in a strange way a positive refuge for me. The imminent danger that we were in at South Park did not come to fruition until about six months later. It was one of those L.A. scorchers of over 90 degrease in May. We were on the Black Top going at it along with several other ball players. This particular day was a Saturday afternoon and the park was even busier than usual. There were people on all four courts, people on the grass playing football. There were even young kids on the playground and in the sandbox. There were even people on the baseball diamond. Because it was the weekend, we had my younger cousin Demetrius with us as well. He was standing near the court watching the action.

I was engaged in a fierce pick-up game and so was Ronald. He was on the opposite end of the court playing with the older kids. Just as I was about to take a shot while driving to the basket, we heard the clicking pump then the deafening explosion of a 12 gage shot gun. It was the loudest and scariest sound I had ever heard. "Boom, Boom!" by the time the second shot happened I was already in route speeding in the opposite direction toward the field. When the third shot came I was at top speed when I remembered that my nephew was by the court so I looked back. There were people screaming and running. I had no idea who the shots were aimed at or where they had come from but they sounded extremely close to us. Before I got to the edge of the other side of the grass, I stopped and kneeled down to see where my nephew was. I was not as concerned about Ronald because I knew he was just as spooked as I was, so he would probably have taken off even before I did. As people continued toward the other side of the park in a frenzy, I looked ahead and was relieved to see both Ronald and Demetrius already on the other side of the field.

As the smoke cleared from the blasts, we knew someone was hit but we had no idea who it was at the time. We just gathered ourselves a bit and jogged home. This was only the second time my 6 year old nephew Demetrius had visited us in our new home. He was still in shock. We were almost afraid to tell anyone in our family about the incident, particularly Herman. He was already demanding that we stay out of that park. It was the last time my nephew spent a day with us while we lived in this neighborhood. I don't think he ever really recovered from that traumatic incident. From that moment to well into his adulthood, he always seemed a bit uncomfortable at outdoor social events or cookouts.

I was beginning to think again about my brother's request to stay out of South Park. Later, we learned that three people were hit by buck shots from the shotgun blasts. A neighborhood teenager named Hook was shot in the back that day, along with another teen and a man who was in the middle of a softball game at the time. How crazy is that? To get shot in the behind in the middle of a baseball game while trying to get to second base, is a shame. All of the victims recovered. We also learned that the shooter was there to take revenge on someone who had stolen his radio.

My boycott of South Park only lasted two days. I guess it is true that addictions are stronger than fear. I was so hooked on the game that whenever I went over to South Park, I was literally putting my life at risk. This environment was overwhelmed with gang violence and drug trafficking. South Park at the time was the center piece of a growing turf war between drug dealers.

Although crack and freebasing was just arriving on the scene. The most popular drug at the time was called Sherm. It was in the form of a brown cigarette that was dipped in embalming fluid. This was just before the development of crack cocaine which would soon hit this community like a deadly plague. Sherm sticks as they were called, were sold on the street for about $20 dollars apiece. The drug was a hallucinogen like PCP. The drug dealers who dealt with Sherm would rob funeral homes to obtain the chemicals to make the drug. There was a black family in our neighborhood that owned several liquor stores and a funeral home. They were the victims of a vicious attack at their funeral home that lead to the death of several family members who were operating the business. The incident drew more negative attention to the area of South Central Los Angeles, particularly this neighborhood surrounding South Park.

After several days of abstaining, I figured the park had suffered enough without me being there, so I returned. I was afraid to let the fellows know that I was afraid to come to the park after the shooting so I just lied and said I had been over to my brother's house for the last few days. It was an unwritten rule to never admit when you are scared. Every fool in the park that day was in panic mode like a runaway slave. No one wanted to admit that they were scared to death.

After a couple of usual games of twenty one, which is a popular game where several players can compete with each other individually at the same time, we headed over to the construction site at the park. We were excited to learn that they had started breaking ground to build a new basketball gym in South Park. At that point there were very few places besides schools that had indoor basketball courts. We were even more excited to learn that they were going to include glass backboards which we only saw on T.V. at that time. We were so anxious that we went over there every day to monitor the progress. We would have even pitched in to help build the thing if we could.

On my way home that day, I wondered if we would still be living here by the time the gym would be completed. We had been moving quite regularly and I was hoping we would stay in this place for a while. I had made some friends and begin to feel a part of a neighborhood community. Besides the fact that it was a drug and crime infested war zone, it was a pretty cool place to me.

As I walked across the street and approached my home, my focus had changed to wondering if we had food for dinner. Although she had her moments, my mother when she was not drinking was a nurturer who demonstrated love and responsibility toward her children and household. However, on or around paydays which was either the first or the fifteenth of the month, she was a different person. Lately, my mom had been intoxicated, that there would be no food in the house and no money to get any. Sometimes during this time, my only complete meal would be at school. Naturally, I had a little weight problem, I couldn't gain any. In a twisted kind of way I actually admired fat people. To me it meant they were obviously eating well. That however did not stop me from talking about them. I'd have an array of fat jokes ready for my homeboy Jeffrey who was a bit on the swollen side. He always talked about what magnificent meal his mom hooked him up with last night. Even when we would walk to pick *Chunky Jeff* up on the way to school, he would be sitting in front of a stack of pancakes, eggs and sausages during the week. Most of us would be lucky to get a bowl of cereal in the morning before school.

Although I would tease Jeffrey any chance I get, I envied how his mother would cook for him regularly. I would sometimes walk over to his house when I knew it would be about dinner time. His mother would always ask if I could stay for dinner. She never said anything but I could since that she knew that I was a neglected child.

When I walked into my house, I notice the house was dark. As I attempted to turn on the light, I realized that the power had been turn off. It had not been the first time. We had a couple of flash lights stashed away for the occasion. I saw my mother passed out on the sofa. I could tell she had been drinking, I had seen this picture several times before. I lifted her leg that was hanging off, back on to the sofa, so she wouldn't fall onto the floor.

I looked around in the kitchen for something to eat and found nothing. I looked into the refrigerator hoping to see something other than just an old box of baking soda which is all I saw in there this morning. I closed the refrigerator door disappointed, still hungry and in the dark.

The next day with the help of my sister Cherolyn, we made arrangements to pay the electric bill and power was restored. Although we still had no food, I sat down in the living room to catch some of the Lakers game which usually would take my mind off of my empty stomach. Instead, the first thing that pops on the T.V. is a Sizzler commercial that teases me with images of a juicy steak. This is the last thing you want to see when you are hungry.

Moments later, Ronald comes through the door with a bag full of junk food. As a teenager he had ways of hustling up a few bucks when the need was there. He would play one on one games against kids in the neighborhood for money. He was a pretty good player so he would win money quite often. From his winnings he had purchased chips candy and a soda that he shared with me which was very rare. Ronald was usually one of the stingiest people on the face of the earth. My mother always told us that he was stingy because his ears were extremely small. As a matter of fact she emphasized that's how you determine if a person is generous or not, by the size of their ears.

Well, on this day he knew from the look on my face that I needed something to eat so we shared what was left of his snack food and watched the rest of the Lakers game somewhat satisfied. The small amount of junk food was just enough to sooth the pains of hunger. We were too proud to call someone for assistance when things got this bad. If they became any worse, we would call maybe one person in our lives at the time who was stable enough to do something for us, that was Herman and his wife Jackie. Unfortunately, we were not close or comfortable enough to even reach out to any other family members. Our relationship with our uncles or aunts was almost completely severed at the time.

As a youth worker, I carry this experience with me as I interact with needy families and youth. Some people are too proud or shame to ask for help. A child would certainly be uncomfortable expressing his or her needs that would then expose inadequacy in their home life. Discerning the needs of others in your environment makes you a valuable asset in your community. I have made it part of my life's work to contribute to the wellbeing of youth and families. If I notice a child who is acting out or appears to be neglected in any way, I pay particular attention to that child with intent to find resources to address those needs. You never know who is in need. As a child, I often prayed that someone would offer us some help when things were really bad.

CHAPTER 16

ANOTHER TRAUMATIC TURNING POINT

"It had to be something serious for us to miss school. Normally, you would have to be spitting up blood to miss school in this family."

After a few years living on 51st and Avalon in Los Angeles, the environment would finally directly affect our lives. On a weekend away at my brother Herman's apartment, we received a phone call that startled him as he rushed out of the apartment on a Sunday evening when he would normally use this time to take Ronald and me back home. Although he only communicated with his wife Jackie what was happening, we could sense that it had something to do with our mother. We knew it was serious because it was getting late on a Sunday night and no one seemed to be concerned about the fact that we needed to get home and prepared for school the next day. It had to be something serious for us to miss school. Normally, you would have to be spitting up blood to miss school in this family.

The next day, we only received bits of information that my mother was in the hospital and they would tell us more, later. Meanwhile, each of my adult siblings were very busy mobilizing and planning things that affected me. Things such as, who will I be staying with and what I am going to do about school. This sketchy bit of information mad me even more uneasy. Until I finally literally cried out, "what's going on? Where is mommy!" my emotional outburst interrupted their discussion. After a brief silence, my sister Cherolyn approached me diligently trying to contain her emotions. She couldn't do it. Her eyes swelled with tears as she attempted to comfort me by saying, "it's going to be alright baby." It then hit me that my mother was either, seriously hurt or dead. There was a deep tense and tight pain that surfaced inside me that I had never felt before. I needed more information than that. I responded fighting back tears of my own, "where is she?" After receiving no immediate answer, I lost it. I cried like an infant for several minutes until I was physically and emotionally exhausted.

Finally, they explain to me that she had an accident and that she was still in the hospital resting. While she was in the hospital, I would be staying with my older brother in Topanga Canyon outside of L.A. while she recovers. He made arrangements for me to be home schooled for the last two months of the semester.

Even with that information, I had more questions. Why couldn't I see her? What happened to her? Can I talk to her? None of these questions were answered. What my older siblings did not want to communicate to me obviously for my own benefit at the time, was that something happened to my mother on her way home from paying a bill that caused her to collapse near the park. The medical report indicated that she had a Cerebral Aneurysm and they needed to perform emergency brain surgery or it will be fatal.

The emergency surgery took place at Martin Luther King Jr. Hospital in Los Angeles. My older siblings kept me safely uninformed of how critical my mother's condition was, yet they were bracing themselves to deliver the would be tragic news to me collectively. After the surgery, the doctor delivered the dreadful information to the family that our mother would be either in a coma or vegetative state for the remainder of her life or she would go into respiratory failure at any moment. The prognosis was far from good and the doctors gave us very little reason to be optimistic. My older siblings with their wives and significant others entered the bedside of our mother. My brother Ronald and I were not old enough to be in the room at the time. Children under 13 were not allowed to be in the intensive care unit. As they held hands and prayed over her, fearing the worse from the grim news that was coldly delivered by the doctor just moments earlier, she slightly opened her eyes and asked, "Whatchya'll doing?" in her usual sharp tone. Her sudden conscious response startled those who were present in the room. They quickly summoned for the nurse, who seem just as shocked as she tended to our mother paying close attention to her vital signs.

From that moment, it would be a slow but steady recovery for the woman that has been called a cat with nine lives. It would be nearly a month before

I was allowed to see my mother. Apparently the condition resulted in her being in a coma for several days. Once she regained consciousness they kept her in intensive care for a week longer where no minors were allowed. I later learned that it would have been too much for me to see her in that physical condition at the time. She was almost unrecognizable.

While my mother was in recovery, I spent that time being home schooled by my older brother. He had left UCLA and formed a band called KARAZZ, an R&B and Jazz fusion group that produced a very unique sound. The group consisted of a five piece band and two soulful female vocalist which was his first wife who was a former gospel singer and my sister Cherolyn. My brother Herman and brother-in-law Charles were also in the group. He and a few of the band members rented a summer house in the rural Topanga Canyon area which was about an hour drive from L.A.

Before my mom's incident, we would spend every weekend in Topanga Canyon. I would find a great deal of joy coming home from school on Fridays knowing that as soon as I got home, I would see a red

VW Bug and several other family vehicles waiting for me to get home so we could hit the road in order to beat traffic as we'd head for the mountains. The house was amazing! It was actually a three story cabin style home with a huge creek in the front of it. During the winter season the creek would transform into a beautiful freshwater river that ran rapidly through the Canyon. We would have to create a mini bridge to get from one side to the other. My favorite part of the house was the family room which had a huge room sized sofa that was sunk in, you had to step down into. We would all pile in and sit around watching television and listening to music.

When I was told that I would be staying there for a while, I was not mad at all. I was free from 95th Street Elementary School where I was labeled as a "Lil Nappy headed Tramp". Living in a place where most people would consider a vacation spot or summer camp was a slice of paradise in my mind. The only down side was that for the first time, I would be separated from my Brother Ronald who was in Jr. High School at the time.

During my stay with my older brother and being home schooled in Topanga Canyon, I was introduced to Black Historical figures such as Malcolm X, Thurgood Marshall and Frederick Douglas. During that time, he also instilled in me an appreciation for reading. Thanks to this brother, I also developed a joy for the game of Chess and Jazz music. He would introduce me to Charlie Parker, Dizzy Gilespy and Miles Davis as their music would be playing as background to our study sessions. It was through my older brother, where I begin the process of critical thinking. To this day I believe critical thinking saved my life, along with many more lives more than any other form of protection. Later, this would be even more validated when I learned this scripture from the book of proverbs in the Bible, "When wisdom enters the heart. Thinking ability will safeguard you." I learned more in those few months being home schooled by my older brother than I did in the last three years of elementary school.

When my mother was well enough to be released from the hospital, I returned home. I will never forget how traumatized I was when I was finally allowed to see her. Although my siblings made an effort to prepare me for my mother's physical condition, I was not ready for what I would see.

Over three months had passed and I was excited to see her. As I walked into her room there was a middle aged woman badly bruised, bald, with no teeth. My mother had smooth skin, gorgeous black hair and a bright smile. My reaction to her physical condition was that of a ten year old. When I realized that this was my mother, I once again gave way to tears. This time I was comforted by my mother. She held me and assured me that she was alright and everything would be O.k.

The emergency brain surgery that was performed on her resulted in her having her head shaved. She also lost several of her front teeth. The bruises on her face and upper body would take several months to completely heal. To this day we are not certain what happened to her that night near the park and there were no witnesses. She was apparently found unconscious with physical bruises to her head and upper body. It could have been a collective effect of years of drinking and a history of high blood pressure that caused the aneurysm, or it could have been caused by sudden head trauma. The latter brought even more speculation that something foul took place.

The speculations lead to several unofficial street investigations by certain family members which gave credence to the possibility that my mother had been viciously attacked, beaten and left for dead. Even more troubling was that if an attack did happened, this would have taken place literally across the street from our home in the park where we had spent so much time. Although, South Park was notoriously violent, we were natives and felt reasonably safe there. It would be a mystery in my family history for years into my adulthood. Neither of these questions would be completely answered. My mother has no recollection and our family rarely speaks of the incident.

After the incident with my mother, life would never be the same. She would never fully recover and would be labored with frequent seizures for the rest of her life. She would need constant care and medication for her condition. My relationship and role changed dramatically as we adjusted to her new condition. At age ten, I would be forced into maturity as a monitor and caregiver. She would have these violent Grand Mal seizures that were horrible to witness. She sporadically would have convulsions, ridged muscle stiffness and slip into unconsciousness. Before the doctors could diagnose her epileptic condition, we had no idea what to do or how to treat these seizures that were happening dangerously too frequent.

The first time we witness this was one of the scariest and stressful moments of my life. We were outside observing the usual antics of the drunks and dope fiends across the street in the park. The peculiar behavior of the neighborhood characters provided enough live entertainment to keep you on the edge of your ring side seat across the street. It was a typical summer day in L.A., hellishly hot and smoggy.

As Ronald and I tossed around a small football in the front yard while we monitored the South Park side show, my mother was sitting in a patio chair in the front yard nursing a 12once can of Old English 800. It had been a month or so after she had been released from the hospital. Her recovery had been progressing well in spite of her physical hindrances as a result her surgeries. She was gradually reemerging as her old sharp, witty and sassy self.

Just as I released a spiraled pass, headed toward Ronald, out of the corner of my eyes, I vaguely observed my Mom slowly slide out of her chair. As I quickly reacted, I could see her entire body shacking violently on the grass next to the chair. "Mommy!" I yelled. Ronald, reached her before I did, also, panicking" What's wrong?" We franticly yelled for someone to call an ambulance or get some help. Her body was completely stiffening and her eyes were fixed in their corners. My first emotional fear was that she had been shot. I realized that neither of us heard the all too familiar sound of gun fire. Dismissing that notion I continued searched her body for any blood or visible wounds.

As her body began to slowly relax from the tense convulsive state, a neighbor came over to assist us. The elderly woman explained to us that our mother was having a seizure and there was nothing we can do but allow it to pass and make sure she had nothing in her mouth. Still in a panic, I was still calling out to her and trying to get her off of the ground. Again the neighbor insisted that I not try to move her until the seizure had completely passed. She was still panting and her body was still slightly twitching. It was an absolutely horrible sight, to witness your loved one suffering something like this.

It would be several weeks and multiple visits to the hospital before the doctors would find the suitable medical prescription to subside the seizures. The medication Phenobarbital and Dilantin would be a regular part of our daily necessities. Prior to this, I would have to monitor her closely with a concerning perspective knowing that she would be vulnerable to a seizure for unknown reasons. I would even sleep next to her with my leg touching hers so that I will be awaken by her shaking convulsive body prompting me to take action.

From this point forward, my responsibilities and focus changed dramatically. At age ten, I was responsible for monitoring my mother's daily activities and physical condition. This included providing medication, preparing meals and helping her to get dressed. This sudden condition prompted a secondary health concern. Although she had suffered a serious life threatening incident that caused permanent brain damage, she was also still an alcoholic which compounded the problem.

According to her regular physician, the combination of the type of medication she was taking and the over consumption of alcohol could be fatal.

At this point, we were not sure if our mother had enough value for her life or the desire to live, to make the necessary adjustments to stop drinking. She had certainly lived a reckless life style which has resulted in incarceration, major injuries, failed marriages and the loss of her children which nearly destroyed her entire family. Would the very imminent fear of death from alcohol and prescription drugs be enough for her to change her course?

CHAPTER 17

THE 1ST AND 15TH

*"For us it would be a social disaster if we were to
show up at school or at the park with new shoes on
the 2nd of the month. You would be talked about
teased and embarrassed the entire day."*

Our only form of income at the time was the L.A.
County welfare system which paid the less fortunate
folks like us on the 1st and 15th day of the month.
It was absolutely embarrassing and degrading for
you to reveal that you were a welfare child. Since
my mother did not work, we were dependent on
the system for income, food and medical assistance.
It was a minimum amount of money that barely
allowed you the necessities. What made it worse
was the alcoholism that added neglect and poor
judgment. My mothers' struggles with alcohol would

have her literally out of it and passed out within hours of receiving a check on the 1st or the 15th. By the time she would be done with her drinking binge which would be days later, sometimes there would be no money left for food or utility bills.

The illness of alcoholism would literally abduct our mother for days. She would be missing for several days at a time with no contact. Ronald and I would have to fend for ourselves during her absence for food and household needs. Initially, I would be in tears looking out the window at night wondering where my "Mommy" was. Fearing the worse and dreading to see a police officer approach the door. After the third day with no word from her, Ronald would put her picture in the bible as an act of faith. She would usually be brought home by one of her drinking friends still slightly inebriated. I would never sleep well until she returned so I was obviously at ease to see her come home. Over time, I would get use to her brief disappearances. Once she would return she would be broke, which meant we would be short on funds for food and bills.

We would literally have to steal the money from her sometimes in order to buy groceries or pay bills. It was usually Ronald who would wait until she got drunk enough to pass out then he would sneak the money out of her purse and set some aside for food and bills. My older sisters Cherolyn and Connie who had places and kids of their own, helped make sure that the utilities were paid while Herman would take us grocery shopping. He taught me how to make a little bit of money last.

There were times when we only had about five or ten dollars to get enough food that would last until the next pay day. He would throw in some extra money when he could but most of the time he would give us something more valuable than money—good old common sense and wisdom. He taught us to shop wisely by purchasing things that would last longer. He had the ability to make ten dollars go a long way. A 5lbs bag of rice for $2, a pack of ground beef $3.00, a couple of cans of chili $1.25, a dozen of eggs $1.50, a loaf of bread .75 cent and a pack of lunch meat $1.50. This routine would give us breakfast lunch and dinner for a week.

At age eleven, I had learned this lesson the hard way. Instead of following this shopping advice one day I decided to shop with my eyes instead of my brain.

I was home alone with my mother who was out at the time. Ronald spent the weekend over Herman's house babysitting which was a regular routine. It was rare that one of us would go without the other. My oldest Brother Herman would consistently have us out to his house as much as his wife could stand. It was a nice get-away from the environment both the dangerous neighborhood and the unstable household situation we were in. Herman specifically instructed me to buy some food to last me the weekend and he would bring more groceries back when he brought Ronald home on Sunday night. I had about five dollars to spend on food. I went into the local market and saw a bright and delicious looking T.V. dinner with steak potatoes and a brownie for dessert. I could not resist the urge to taste for the first time a juicy steak almost like the kind that would tease me in the Sizzler commercials. At least that's what it looked like on the box. I gave in, and bought the steak dinner for $2.99 which left me with $2.01. I bought some Kool-Aid and a small box of sugar to complete my shopping spree.

I ate well that Friday night but was hungry again by Saturday morning.

With my mom still gone, I was on my own as far as trying to find a meal for the rest of the day. When the hunger pains got to be too much for me, I mustered up enough nerve to go next door to ask the neighbor for an egg. I simply lied by saying that my mother is baking a cake and needed an egg. Ms. Helen probably knew darn well that my mother was in no condition to be baking a cake. It was no secret to anyone in the neighborhood that my mother was an alcoholic. Just as I had hoped she gave me not one but two eggs. I use the same line with Ms. Liz who lived in the back of us but added that we also needed a cup of milk. I now had four eggs and a cup of milk. I used the milk as a mixer to the eggs to add more as I scrabbled them. The watered down eggs lasted me till Saturday night. By the time Sunday evening came I was so hungry my stomach was rubbing my back. I settled my stomach a little by eating lemons from a tree behind Ms. Liz's house. Although I had never done it before, I even ate the inside of the lemon which provided a little lining for my stomach. I darn near even ate the peels and all. When my brothers came through the door with bags of food, I felt like doing cart wheels in the living room.

My periodic hunger pains would propel me into maturity at age eleven. I would find various ways to earn money. Not for candy and snacks but for basic necessities that normally is provided by adults. Mainly, I would wash people cars for a few bucks at a time. Although I was a bit raggedy I was still kind of a cute kid. One of my mother's drinking buddies was a custodian who would often bring us discarded items from the buildings that he worked in. Quite often we would keep the pencils and various school supplies for ourselves but on this occasion he brought a huge box of small Spanish books. Ronald and I first thought we'd just toss them in the garbage being that we couldn't read them. The next day, I decided to take them next door to our Spanish neighbors instead of dumping them. When I approached the neighbors, the first question they asked was how much? I actually had no initial intention of actually selling them but my thoughts changed quickly. "about a dollar a piece", I suggested. In just a few moments my generous gesture turned into a business transaction resulting in $11 dollars. "Cha Ching!"

I returned home budding with excitement and eager to repeat my business venture with more of my Spanish folks in the hood. I still had plenty of books left in the box. I even sold a few to the local liquor store workers who was impressed at my salesmanship enough to buy the remainder of the books from me. At the end of the day I earned $23 dollars. I used the money wisely taking my older brothers advice by buying enough food for about two weeks. I also bought enough *Now & Laters* to keep me smiling for just as long.

Although most people in the neighborhood were either below middle class or on a fixed income, they went through great lengths to try to conceal the fact that they were on welfare. On occasion my mother would purchase us new cloths when she received a check on the 1st of the month. To avoid exposure and a great deal of embarrassment, I wouldn't wear the cloths for several days or even a week later. She could not understand why I wouldn't wear those brand new cloths she just bought me. For a youth at this time, it would be a social disaster if we were to show up at school or at the park with new shoes on the 2nd of the month. You would be talked about teased and embarrassed the entire day. Every kid in the neighborhood would be calling you a welfare child or county boy. I would sometimes try to intentionally make the shoes look worn down or dirty. It was extremely stressful for me.

I had made that mistake about a year before when my mother purchased me a pair of athletic shoes from the local grocery store. The shoes were an imitation version of Nikes with the upside down swooshes. I was obviously ignorant of modern fashion or popular brands at the time because I actually wore these shoes to school thinking they were Nikes and instantly became the joke of the day. It was so bad that several kids were literally following me around campus just to laugh and make jokes about me. "Deon, has on some upside down Nikes." I finally got fed up, smacked one kid in the mouth and ran home. On the way home, I dumped those shoes into a garbage can in the alley behind our apartment. Not wanting to ever step foot in that school environment again, I played sick for the next several days. I told my mother that someone had stolen my shoes at school during P.E. I don't know how she fell for that one. Who in the world would steal some upside down Nikes? I actually should have taken Ronald's hint when he asked me, "you're not gonna wear those to school are you?" I see now that he was trying to warn me of what I'd be getting into by stepping on the school yard with some fake Nikes.

I also avoided the free meal line in school throughout Jr. High & High School. I almost never ate lunch during those times. It was amazing that the school administrators did not realize how it exposed so many students to social ridicule and embarrassment. They also issued reduced priced meal tickets that the kids quickly labeled "county tickets" which gave the meal tickets a negative stigma. Years later, the public school system in California made the necessary adjustments to reduce the stigma attached to underprivileged students who was eligible for free or reduced lunch.

This is evident of how critical it is to embrace and understand a child's social environment. Today's modern youth generation is suffering from an alarming increase in teen suicides. Many youth service professionals believe it is the social pressures coupled with the lack of nurturing relationships that is the main contributor to the deadly trend. By being socially disconnected, my mother had no idea how miserable it was for us. In my current capacity, I have worked with youth who have admitted to participating in illegal activities to obtain money for basic needs. One particular student shared with me how she became involved in a ring of stealing from department stores in order to sell stolen products to earn enough money to participate in her senior activities such as homecoming, prom and senior pictures. She was an honor student who was arrested and incarcerated for several months which ruined her entire senior year. There is no justification for illegal activities and reckless behavior, however adult supervision and home stability could deter many youth from making bad decisions. This is why youth employment development programs are so critical to the community. As a youth career development trainer, it is empowering to help youth become employable, productive citizens.

Not having a home telephone was also something that caused me unnecessary stress. A landline is a basic household need that was not available in my life. My worse nightmare at the time was for a girl to ask me for my phone number which was about as likely as catching a unicorn during a snow storm in L.A. If such an unlikely event where to occur, it would be humiliating to have to tell her that I don't have a phone. This wouldn't be so rare if this was the 1950s but it was 1980 and it seemed like every household but ours had a phone at home.

Not having name brand clothes was just as painful. Not expensive designer jeans such as *Jordash* or *Guess* which was popular brands at the time but common brands such as *Levi* jeans. I was the only twelve year old boy still wearing tough skins jeans to school. These were jeans with the build in knee pads that were designed for younger boys who were rough on clothes.

There was absolutely nothing attractive about me whatsoever at the time. My hair was so thick and nappy that even a medal cake cutter type of afro comb, could not cut through it. I could get hit in the head with a rock and I wouldn't feel a thing. I was dusty, raggedy and still did not care too much about my appearance. When in most cases at age 12, boys begin to be very self-conscious. I couldn't care less. Give me a pack of Now & Laters and a basketball and I was at peace with the world.

Ronald, however, diligently guarded his physical appearance and reputation. He would give out my brother Herman's phone number as his own. He would make sure his hair was just right and he tried hard to keep up with the latest fashion trends. We had no iron, so he would lay out his clothes for the next day then lay them down flat in between his mattress and the box spring so they would be wrinkle free in the morning. Hey, it beats using a hot rock as an iron. The Flintstones were more advanced than us.

Once in a while, we would have to go get my mother from a local bar or from one of her drinking buddy's house when she would be too intoxicated to walk home. It was quite embarrassing to have to almost carry her down the street when she'd have too much to drink. Ronald would conveniently not be available most of the time for this task. One of his greatest fears was to be seen by one of his classmates with our mother in this condition. It would be an instant image and reputation killer. He would have to change schools.

We rarely brought anyone to the house for obvious reasons. We had a glass window pane front door that was trimmed with wood. I'm not sure if the designer of this place really thought this through. Who in their right mind would have a glass door in the ghetto? And, no it was not that protective glass you see in the banks or at 7 Eleven. We may as well have just left the door wide open. Within a year, for various reasons, several of the glass window panes were broken. There were so many holes in this door we never needed a key to get in the house. All we had to do was stick our arm through one of the empty pains and unlock the door. We would come into the house using our arm as the key and my slightly inebriated mother would have the nerve to say, "lock that dow!" There was absolutely no sense of security whatsoever. Fear and discomfort often prevented me from sleeping at night.

CHAPTER 18

REFUGE ON THE COURT

"I have several childhood pictures of me with a green striped shirt and a short thick nappy afro, looking like Ernie from Sesame Street."

The challenge of growing through my teen years continued to be further complicated by my dysfunctional home environment. The social issues with peer pressure became a dreadful combination for me. Having an alcoholic mother made me the subject of every jokester around the neighborhood or in school. When my mother's illness became public knowledge around the way, my reputation continued to decline, along with my self-esteem.

Unfortunately, this was also the time and age when your physical appearance was as important as breathing. There were times when I didn't even have a descent pair of basketball shoes. My wardrobe was absolutely pitiful. I was always a relatively short kid so I pretty much stayed the same size from grade school through Jr. High School with no real growth spurt. This also meant I would be wearing the same clothes as I wore in grade school. I'm quite sure I was the only kid still wearing tough skins in 7th grade. I have several childhood pictures of me with a green striped shirt and a short thick nappy afro, looking like Ernie from Sesame Street.

It was extremely difficult to maintain any type of normal childhood in this situation. I could never afford the cost to participate in any organized youth sports activities. Given our hardship circumstances, I couldn't think of asking my mother or anyone else for money for anything outside of the bare necessities like food, clothing or shelter. These were the things that we were barely provided. Fifty or sixty dollars for a baseball or basketball team was out of the question.

There was an exhibition game set up for the regular young ball players of South Park and a well-organized team from the Baldwin Park area of L.A.

on the upscale west side. I was so excited to be in a somewhat organized basketball game with officials. It was an outdoor game set up by the South Park director Dan. He threw us some old jersey shirts that smelled like they had been locked in an attic for several years but it didn't matter to us. We were just as excited as if they were brand new. There is something very special about putting on a uniform for the first time. You can be a dominant ball player during pickup games but until you can shine in an organized basketball competition, you are just another street ball player. I was looking forward to becoming an official ball player by being on an organized team.

I was so excited that I couldn't wait to get started. As soon as the ball was tossed up and tapped, I was right there to intercept the ball and take it in for a lay-up. My brother Ronald who was just three years older than me was the stand in coach which meant we had no faith or respect in his coaching skills so we really didn't listen to him. We just hit the black top and played our game. Without receiving any instruction or guidance, I was in a full court press. I was so charged up that I was attacking every ball handler that touched the ball, creating several steals and easy lay-ups. The other team's coach called a time out to adjust to the pressure. I didn't let up, I was all over the place on both offense and defense.

My older brother, slash Coach was trying to get me to slow it down. I was so caught up into the competition that I didn't want to hear anything from him. I only knew of one way to play and that's full speed. I even told him to sit down and shut up. If we had a sub he probably would have taken me out of the game. It was a good thing that we only had five players. I would have tried to kill him if he had taken me outta that game.

We played two 20 minute halves that seemed to fly by so fast I thought we had another half to play. I scored the majority of the points for our team and had several steals and rebounds. Although it was an excruciatingly hot day, I could have played all day. It was a very competitive game that we ended up losing by 1 point. I was so frustrated with the loss, I was almost in tears. My competitive spirit and zeal to win was obvious.

After the game, I was approached by a middle aged man who watched the game. He was apparently impressed with my passion and energy out there, "Hey kid, you played a helluva game. Don't worry about it. You'll gettm next time. This is for you." He gave me a handshake with a five dollar bill. I looked at him to see if it was really for me. His wink confirmed that it was as I smiled, "Thanks" The pain of losing begin to fade away as my focus quickly changed to how much candy I could buy with this five bucks. Before I hit the store I wisely thought that this money may have to provide dinner at home. I remember the lesson from my older brother who encouraged me to think of what you need before what I want.

Our little pickup group of young players was impressive enough for Mr. Dan to start talking about starting an official South Park Team. That experience also taught me that you never know who's watching when you play, so play hard every time you step out on the court. That unofficial scrimmage game also resulted in me earning a reasonable amount of respect from the kids in the neighborhood even the older ones started giving me *what's up* head nods. I was officially a respected ball player like my older brother Ronald who had made his mark as a flashy hoopster at Bethune Jr. High School.

I had begun to draw the attention of some neighborhood coaches and adults who saw something in my efforts on the basketball court. I was invited to try out for a traveling team at the Queen Ann community center. I made the team among several other pretty good ball players. After the tryout period and cuts were made, the coach asked me to step into the office. He informed me that I had made the team and the cost to participate was $55. He may as well have cut me from the team. Just as excited and uplifted as I was when he told me that I made the team, I was just as disappointed and defeated when he mentioned the cost.

My walk home was filled with mixed emotions. I was both proud yet dejected at the thought of making a very competitive traveling team, yet not being able to participate due to the fee. I almost got the nerve to ask my brother Herman for the money to play but at the same time our electricity was shut off for lack of payment. Again, he had to come to the rescue to deliver us out of literal darkness which we had been in for several days. So, there went that option. I finally gave up on the basketball team and the $55 fee which seemed impossible at the time.

After missing practice for several days, I received a surprise visit from the coach who could not have shown up at a worse time. It was a Saturday afternoon and my mother was groggy from her meds and laying partially unconscious with a crooked wig tilted on her head like a big brim hat. Coach George tapped on the partially opened door, "Hello", as I got up to meet him he was nearly already inside. Attempting to hide my embarrassment I responded, "Oh, hey coach". He subtlety glanced around and asked, "I just came to check on you. We haven't seen you at practice lately." The strange male voice must have awakened her as my mother rose up, "Who is that?" Still slightly out of it, she tried to gather herself and focus. Coach George reached out to introduce himself, "My name is George. I'm a basketball coach at the community center. Deon is on one of our teams." She slurred, "I don't know nothing about Deon being on no *Baseball* team." Although I hoped she wouldn't, she continued, "I got nine cheerin and that's my baby, . . ." she ramble on for minutes then begin to cry.

Coach George recognized how embarrassing this was to me and just said, "Hey Deon, don't worry about a thing, just try to make it to practice tomorrow. Good night Ms. Carrie." Just that quick she had faded back into unconsciousness. He waved at me and stepped out of the raggedy door. I wasn't quite sure what he meant by, "Don't worry about a thing." Obviously, I had plenty to be concerned about. I was a severely under privileged, impoverished kid living in a drug & crime infested neighborhood.

The next day at practice I was prepared to go in to tell Coach George and Coach Mike that I had to quit the team. As I walked into the gym Coach George gestured to me to step into his office. Without saying a word, he just pointed to the desk where there was a new black uniform which was an exact replica of the San Antonio Spurs NBA team as well as a brand new pair of Black and white Leather high top Nikes. My eyes lit up with pleasure as he winked and said again, "Don't worry about the fee." Those words relieved me of so much stress over the last several days, I felt like giving the guy a hug. He later privately asked me to keep this between us. He had seen my home condition, recognize that I was a kid who needed a break and waived the $55 dollar fee.

Being on that team provided me with an opportunity to be exposed to different places throughout Southern California. We traveled to neighborhoods and different cities around the greater Los Angeles area. We played in some of the biggest tournaments and some of the best basketball venues in L.A. including Poly Pavilion at UCLA and ultimately the Fabulous Forum in Inglewood which was the home of the World Champion Los Angeles Lakers. Our coach emphasized to us that we represented not only the Queen Ann community center but we represented a section of L.A. that some people considered a breeding ground for trouble makers and so-called lowlifes. He drilled us on how critical it was for us to dispel those negative stereotypes that tainted the African American community. Some 30 years later, as a basketball coach, I use the same approach while working with young players from notorious communities in the Bay Area such as East Palo Alto, East Oakland and Bay View San Francisco. There are a variety of life skills to learn in youth sports. My first youth basketball coach set a fine example for me that I use to this day as a youth worker and in my capacity as a High School basketball coach.

As a member of this youth basketball program, as part of our challenge we were also instructed to wear collared shirts to every game until we were later provided with team sweat suits. We were not to use profanity whatsoever and was encouraged to conduct ourselves with dignity and respect. If we were to violate this agreement we were not to travel to the next game. As a young player with no father figure, this set of rules was a much needed presence of discipline for me as well as for most of my team mates.

Being a respected athlete, provided me with a protective shield from most of the neighborhood issues that other people suffered and feared. In the mists of an environment that consisted of robberies, attacks and drive by shootings, the athletes were protected. I received an unofficial pass from the drug dealers, gang members and thugs. Once they knew that I was an athlete they were cool with me. They didn't bother me and they would even come to my defense if necessary. Fortunately, I never had to play that card, but it made me a lot more secure to knowing that I had it.

CHAPTER 19

GROUND ZERO OF THE CRACK EPIDEMIC

". . . not only was I paranoid about crack heads or drive by shooters. I also had to be on the lookout for the overzealous L.A.P.D."

In my experience, the vilest period in L.A. was during the height of the crack epidemic during the mid-eighties. Many have voiced their opinion about the worst time to be in Los Angeles. With all due respect to the turbulent times during the civil rights movement which resulted in the Watts Riots in 1965 and the 1992 Riots from the nationally televised notorious L.A.P.D. beating of motorist Rodney King, the impact of Crack trumps them both.

The 1965 riots in Los Angeles were ignited by the arrest of a 21 year old African American motorist, Marquette Frye who was suspected of being intoxicated. A crowd of witnesses accused the officers of using unnecessary force and violence erupted throughout the Watts section of Los Angeles. My family lived in the area during this time. According to my older brothers, this White Police Officer actually pulled the young African American woman out of her car by her hair. This incident, combined with escalating racial tensions, overcrowding in the neighborhood, and a summer heat wave, sparked violence on a massive scale. Many people still believe that the incident alone may not have caused such a massive public reaction without a series of perceived injustices against African Americans.

The Los Angeles Riots of 1992 were sparked when a jury acquitted four police officers who were accused in the videotaped beating of African American motorist Rodney King following a high-speed chase. The urban African American community was appalled. Not so much about the beating. That was no surprise to L.A. natives but the fact that they accused King of speeding over 120mph-IN A HYUNDAI! Really?

After the verdict, thousands of people in the Los Angeles area rioted over a period of six days. Widespread looting, assault, arson and murder occurred while property damages totaled over a billion dollars. In all, 53 people were killed during the riots. Many other factors were cited as reasons for the unrest, including extremely high unemployment among African Americans due to a nation-wide recession; a long-standing perception that the Los Angeles Police Department engaged in racial profiling and use of excessive force. There was also a public rage over the inexcusable sentence of community service which was given to a female Korean American shop-owner for the killing of 13 year old African American girl, Latasha Harlins. Around the same time there was also considerable backlash for the long term sentencing of a black man for kicking a (police)dog.

With respect to the magnitude of these tragic yet historic incidents, including the Northridge earthquake in 1994, I believe the Crack Epidemic was the worst thing to ever happen to the City of

Los Angeles. Considering the long term effect, death toll from the violence associated with the drug wars, the social economic impact and subsequent destruction of the family, nothing has caused as much long term devastation to multiple generations as Crack. In most cases during this time and environment, the fathers were out of the picture for various reasons. Suddenly, Crack is introduced to mainly the urban African American community. Due to easy access and affordability, Crack particularly attracted vulnerable black females. The potency made it one of the most addictive drugs up to that time which debilitated the person's ability to make rational decisions. The constant pursuit of the initial high exhausted all aspects of a person's desire to maintain personal responsibility. As a result, children were being neglected, woman prostituting themselves as favors to support their drug habit. People were stealing and selling anything of value to cop a few pieces of "rock cocaine". I witnessed a person selling his car for $20 worth of Crack and a person running down the street with a fully decorated Christmas Tree that they had stolen out of someone's house. These strange behaviors were unprecedented yet they quickly became quintessential behaviors of a "Crack Head". It was desperate times where people would sell just about anything to get or stay high. Before Crack, or as Dr. Joe Marshall puts it, BC, a person had to have a decent amount of money to get high. Cocaine or heroin was relatively expensive but a person could obtain Crack for as little as $10-$20. It seemed like instantly, everyone was high on Crack at this time.

I vividly remember being startled at approximately 3am in the morning during high school. I could hear someone scuffling around in the house. Assuming it was my mother or brother Ronald, I initially blew it off as nothing and tried to resume catching my much needed Z's. Wait! I thought. Ronald is in Compton and I could hear my mom in her bed calling the hogs (snoring). Then! Who in the hell is that? I grabbed a bat from my closet and slowly moved toward the sound. I approached the sound to discover that it was a Crack head who had broken into our house. He was in the kitchen cooking an omelet as if he lived there. "What the *%*$*??? I startled him by yelling and swinging the bat toward him as I chased him out of the house. Although I was a pretty good athlete running a 4:6 forty yard dash, I could not catch this guy. Never underestimate the quickness of a Crack head.

Unfortunately, I was attending high school during these trying times. Due to the drug wars associated with the influx of Crack in the community, the environment was saturated with violence by-way of drive by shootings, home invasions and carjacking's which became more prevalent during this time.

Street Gangs has been a part of L.A. since the early 1970s. There has been a presence of Crips and Bloods for decades in Southern California. However, before Crack there was a certain amount of loyalty and unity between Crips and Bloods. After Crack or AC, it no longer mattered. Crips were killing Crips and Bloods were killing Bloods. It seemed as though there was a murder or drive by shooting on a daily basis. There were so many murders during this time that the Los Angeles Police Department under the direction of controversial L.A.P.D. Chief of Police Daryl Gates would no longer investigate the incident. It was written off as a "Gang related" murder which at the time did not have high priority of being solved.

Daryl Gates was appointment as Chief in conjunction with the intensification of the War On Drugs. A drug-related issue that had also come to the forefront at the time was gang violence, which paralyzed many of the neighborhoods particularly the Black and Hispanic communities in which gangs had a strong hold. In response, the L.A.P.D. set up specialist gang units which gathered intelligence on and ran operations against gangs. These units were called Community Resources against Street Hoodlums, aka CRASH. Gates' aggressive approach to the drug gang problem resulted in allegations of false arrest and a general L.A.P.D. disregard for young Black and Latino men were made. By this time however, the department had a significant percentage of minority officers.

Gates himself became a byword among some for excessive use of force by anti-gang units, racial profiling and became a favorite target for critics. The popular L.A.P.D.. slogan became *"to serve, protect and break a niggas neck"* which was in response to the infamous choke hold implemented that used the PR-24 (night stick) that resulted in many *accidental* deaths. Nevertheless, CRASH's approach appeared successful and remained in widespread use until the negative attention to the abuses of the law threatened to undo hundreds of criminal convictions.

It is safe to say that Los Angeles was a hot mess and I wanted out. So, not only was I paranoid about crack heads or drive by shooters. I also had to be on the lookout for the overzealous L.A.P.D. who was just looking to take in or take out a young black boy whom they assume were all up to no good. Hip hop artist Ice cube of the group NWA (Niggas With Attitudes) put it best in the rap tune, "F" The police—"Messing with me cause I'm a teen-ager. With a little bit of gold and a pager . . ." All I wanted at this time was to "get the hell out of L.A" and as my mother would say "quick, fast and in a hurry".

My focus during my Junior year became how in the hell am I going to get out of L.A. Between the winos and crack heads in and around my life, I had begun to lose all since of respect for the adults in my life. I had just chased a crack head out of my own kitchen and my mother's alcoholism and medical condition had all but made her dysfunctional at this time. Basically, I was on my own, which meant I had to summon enough self-discipline and internal motivation to reach my primary objective of surviving this extremely unhealthy environment and separating from it. The question was . . . . how? Army? College? Or Job?

CHAPTER 20

ESCAPE FROM L.A.

"He took my jacket. He took my money. He even took my Chicken. Which was extremely evil? He had the money! He could have at least left me something to eat."

During this turbulent time in the city of angels, my biggest fear was the potential violence that could erupt on any given Sunday or any other day of the weekday or night. The beauty and tropical surroundings of L.A. can and often does deceive people. The palm trees, green manicured lawns and one level houses may present a delusion of a peaceful neighborhood. Most inner city hoods actually look the part of the traditional Ghetto with run down public housing projects with boarded up buildings and abandoned cars. Although there are housing projects in certain areas and locations that are eye sores, L.A is relatively nice looking even in the most crime infested areas. However, do not let it fool you. The nicest looking neighborhood could be the worst area's to live in.

The constant stories of gang violence, drive by shootings, carjackings and home invasions was only further validated by personal experience and witnessing it for myself. My first experience with violence during this time was during the ninth grade. I was on my way home from school after basketball practice. I was crossing Jefferson Avenue when a car full of what appeared to be gang members rolled by. Being a teenager in a relatively new neighborhood was a danger at this time. Quite often there were senseless killings of innocent young people for simply being in the wrong place at the wrong time. There was so very little regard for life that it didn't matter if you were a rival gang member or not. You would be shot just because.

So needless to say, I was quite alarmed when I was startled by a slow creeping vehicle rolling beside me on the street. Living in an environment where drive by shootings occur on a daily basis, you develop certain instincts like, keeping your eyes open and being aware of your surroundings at all times. There was a saying at the time . . . "Stay alert! Stay alive!" You also learned to carry yourself in a non-threatening way yet not appear to be a walking victim.

As the car approached me, I was mindful but I didn't want to appear too fearful or startled, although I was shaking in my sneakers with fear. I slowly turned to see what I feared the most which was a car full of knucklehead thugs just looking for trouble. If I was a target they would have just blasted me right away. But this must have been a gang initiation where the recruits had to get their hands dirty. One hooded fella on the passenger side yelled out "What set you from cuzz?" When you hear this, it doesn't matter what comes out of your mouth. They have already made up their mind that you were going to be their next victim. At this point, I'm thinking, escape route so I distracted them by dropping my back pack and cutting across their vehicle and on to the busy intersection of Jefferson Blvd. I knew at least one or two of them would go after the back pack although there was nothing but some funky sweat socks in it, giving me more time to put distance between us. I heard them struggling to get out of the car as I dashed across the busy street causing several cars to slam on their breaks and blow their horns. Question to self: would you rather be hit by a car or shot? I was running on pure adrenalin and fear as I flashed to the other side of the street and down another side street.

I could hear the screeching of the car trying to adjust to pursue me. My heart was pounding through my chest as I darted through an apartment complex and down a second street. I took another quick shortcut through the alley and hopped a gate of an old house. In the backyard was a small tree house. I climbed the tree and rested in the small wooded flat for a good while until I was sure that the would be attackers were long gone. By the time I left the tree house to head back home it was dark. Better safe than dead.

My understanding of this environment was that anyone could be shot and killed at any time for any reason. There was very little regard or value for life in Los Angeles at this time. The homicide rate per capita was one of the highest in the country. With this, constantly on my mind, obviously a touch of paranoia set in. I would never go to too many social events either formal or informal with the fear of potential violence.

As a youth life skills coach, I often share with young people to . . . "not be afraid of fear". As in my case, fear can be a valuable asset to you. I'm not sure if I would have survived living in such an environment had it not have been for the protection of fear. In 1984, I was invited to a house party on 54th street. At this time the biggest and most ruthless gang was the Rollin 60s. So when I was asked to attend a house party after a high school football game on 54th street, it was fear that helped me draw the conclusion that "Hey, 54th street is pretty close to 60 . . . I'm not going." My peers were teasing me about being "scared" or a "punk". My thought was . . . they could call me whatever they wanted to. I couldn't care less. I was not going to a house party on 54th street. More than likely there will be some "Rollin 60s" there looking for trouble. The ridicule from my so-called homeys continued but it failed to persuade me. I made my way home hoping they would change their minds.

Later in the evening, my mother called me into the living room. Something had happened. As we drew our attention to the small black and white T.V. with aluminum foil around the antenna for better reception, the news telecast validated what I had feared. There was live footage of the aftermath of a shooting. Eleven teenagers were shot and five of them were killed in what would be called the 54th street massacre. Apparently, some unwanted guests arrive and were turned away. These suspected gang members return and opened fire on the very party that I was invited to. Luckily, none of my friends were among the injured or dead but it was yet another valuable lesson on trusting your instincts and fear.

Nature teaches us the valuable lesson of knowing when to adjust to your environment. If it is freezing temperature outside, you need to adjust by wearing the appropriate winter clothing. If the temperature is over 100 degrees, you need to adjust to it by removing layers of clothes to avoid heat injuries. Survival depends on how well we adjust to a changing environment. This survival instinct of mine was not developed naturally, I learned from experience. By not monitoring my environment, I became a casualty of this environment on several occasions.

The summer of 1984 was a very extraordinary time for the City of Los Angeles. The City was hosting the XXIII Olympiad during the most violent time, a crime wave and the start of the crack epidemic. The world was watching with all eyes on Los Angeles during the most vulnerable period in its existence. Under the direction of the controversial Chief of Police Daryl Gates, the L.A.P.D. went to great lengths to clean up the city from its most notorious criminals.

It was also a fortunate time for the city's economy. The Olympics generated new employment opportunities for many L.A. youth including myself. I was working for Kentucky Fried Chicken on Olympic boulevard. With my first paycheck I bought myself a brand new red 76ers starter jacket which was one of the hottest fashion items at the time, next to the $75 top ten basketball shoes.

I was on my way home on the RTD bus after work at 10:30pm. It was payday on a Friday night so I was feeling pretty good. I had $71.55 in my pocket, I had my bright red 76ers jacket and I had some of the Colonel's extra crispy chicken thighs. It was all good! Until, I got closer to my exit near Jefferson Ave. As the bus stopped, I notice several gangsters standing in the Church's Chicken parking lot on Western and Jefferson. They were just hanging in front of their cars blasting music.

One of them was a notorious neighborhood thug, street named "Moon" who had a reputation for bullying and robbing usually vulnerable individuals like teenagers and senior citizens. He noticed me on the bus and immediately started making his way toward the bus. While the bus door opened to let passengers in or out, he quickly stepped on the bus and walked to the back where I was sitting. He approached me aggressively grabbing my jacket with both hands. "What's up with the Red jacket cuz?" I struggled but I managed to remove his hands from my jacket. He responded by pulling a handgun from his back pocket. It was a slightly rusted black revolver with a brown handle. He shoved the weapon into my belly. As the metal barrel scraped my rib cage, I stepped back in retreat. He took my jacket. He took my money. He even took my Chicken. Which was extremely evil? He had the money! He could have at least left me something to eat.

There were several passengers on the bus at the time. When he had robbed me of my personal items, he simply walked out the back door of the bus that was conveniently waiting while he did the crime. When he stepped out, the driver pulled away as if nothing happened. Besides a few sympathetic glances and heads shaking with pity, not one passenger said or did anything to come to my aid. No one even suggested the driver call dispatch for the police. Probably because it would have been a waste of breathe to do so at the time.

From that moment on, my level of urban consciousness increased even more. I became extremely cautious of where I went, what I was wearing and who I was with. I became almost paranoid when I was in unfamiliar territory. Unfortunately, my troubles would only get worse as my family situation continued to deteriorate.

CHAPTER 21

THE HOOVER PLAZA

"you can always tell a good neighborhood by the address. Anytime you have a fraction in the address; It's bad."

We were constantly moving from place to place throughout my grade school and middle school years. I constantly changed schools. I made the decision that no matter what or where we moved to, I was not changing high schools. I was developing an identity at Dorsey High as an athlete and unique personality. I had a solid group of friends and had earned a measure of respect on campus. Although I was unaware of it at the time, the most critical years in the life of an adolescent is between the ages between 14-17 in particular. This is where most individuals are molded with the characteristics that will eventually develop into the type of adult that they will become.

Although my personal life was quickly deteriorating, I was doing my best to maintain my public or social life by participating in sports and other school activities. I also knew I had to maintain a decent grade point average if I wanted to leave Los Angeles by going to college. I needed to be qualified for admission to a four year college or university and I didn't care which one, as long as it was far enough away from L.A. I would have been happy going to *"Ottisburg"* University in South Dakota, if it even exists.

I was not surprised when my mother informed me that we had to move again. We had been evicted several times before and this time around I had gotten use to the routine. We usually would have to temporarily live with a family member or one of my older siblings but this time my older brother Herman was already on the case as usual and had found us a place on the other side of town. I was almost afraid to ask where we were moving this time.

In L.A. you can always tell a good neighborhood by the address. "23 Palm Avenue" is in a good neighborhood. It even sounds good. If the address is "4353 and 1/3rd C, 298th street", It's usually a horrible area, deep in the hood. Anytime you have a fraction in the address it's bad. That means people living on top of people. I'd hate to be a mailman in the ghetto. You have to know fractions.

We actually moved on 80th and Hoover in South Central L.A. in a two bedroom apartment right near busy Hoover Street called the Hoover Plaza. The area was notorious for drug activities from the Hoover Crips street gang. Moving into a new neighborhood as a black male teen could not only be challenging but right out dangerous. Walking in this hood not knowing anyone was a bad idea. I would now have to take the bus from Dorsey High which is on the west side of L.A. after football or basketball practice, to the other side of town. Practice was out at about 6:30pm. I would literally have to change cloths. I couldn't wear anything with Dorsey on it. Why? Dorsey High is right next to the *jungle* which was an area on the west side known for Blood territory. Any assumed affiliation with a rival gang could get you on the wrong end of a drive by shooting. I couldn't wear blue or red either due to gang affiliation, so I usually just turned my green and white Dorsey hooded sweat shirt inside out. I would not get home until about 8:30 or 9pm.

By me being the new guy, I was at risk walking through this hood, occupied by a notorious street gang called the Hoover Crips. The streets were busy around this time of night with crack heads and drug dealers present doing illegal business. I could often hear gun fire in the near area which was as common as the faint sound of sirens from emergency vehicles or police helicopters in the sky. As I would approach the main boulevard after exiting the bus, I would become anxious and nervous as I carefully scanned the surrounding area. My heart would speed up and I began breathing fast, slowly having a mild anxiety attack as I approached the streets with uncertainty. As I turned down 79th street, I noticed several people interacting, about half the block down the street. Before they noticed me, I quickly cut through an alley behind an apartment complex where I would make my way down to my building. The alley was even darker and anyone could have jumped out on me this time of night but it wasn't nearly as scary as walking through a gauntlet of ruthless young gang bangers with no value for life. I'd rather take my chances with Jason Voorhees, Michael Myers and Freddy Krueger.

This was unfortunately my routine on a daily basis. There was a repeat of the same stress and panic attack every single day. There were times that I would intentionally pass my exit one, sometimes two bus stops away just to avoid the possible confrontation with street thugs on 80th and Hoover. Some evenings, I would consider just staying on the bus until I reached the end of the line wherever that was, just to avoid the fear and stress.

Once I reached my ground floor apartment, the anxiety would subside just a bit. I would usually be too tired to even engage with my mother. She would most of the time have something prepared for dinner but at this point in my life I needed more emotional nourishment. Although she was aware of the grave danger that we were surrounded by, she had no idea how it was effecting me. She figured as long as I wasn't involved in a gang or drugs I was o.k. She had no idea how wrong that thought process was. Like many parents who are several generations older than their children, she was completely disconnected to the issues that her teenaged son was experiencing.

I would settle down in my room. My room windows were facing the busy Hoover Street where I could hear every activity that occurred at all hours of the night. There were drug deals, prostitution and violence nonstop. As it is in many urban communities, you almost become callous or immune to the effects of violence when it happens so frequently.

One late night I was abruptly awaken by gun fire that sounded extremely close to my window. I quickly hopped onto the floor in front of my bed. Moments later, I could hear emergency vehicles and police activity just outside my window. Most of the apartment complex was now outside the building observing what had happened. I watched from my window as the police covered a young black man who had been shot several times. He died just a few feet from my bedroom window. The yellow tarp covered most of his body but I could tell that he was a young black male, probably in his late teens or early 20s. For whatever reason, this was someone's son or brother who will not be coming home. That image of death would haunt me for several months as I realized how easily that could have been me lying dead on the same street that I reluctantly walk down every day. After that eerie evening, I no longer slept in my bed. I would put my mattress on the floor in front of my bed slightly tilted up to block possible stray bullets that could come through my wall or window from busy and deadly Hoover Street.

The Hoover Plaza was a Mecca for drug dealers in the area. A third of the entire 21 unit complex was drug distribution units. Seven apartments all on the top floors were either selling crack or weed. There were at least two armed gang members at the front entrance and two around the back at all hours of the night. We would see them casually walking around with weapons, hand guns and shotguns. Sometimes they wouldn't even bother to conceal them.

Just when we thought we had experienced the worst, after seeing someone shot to death under my window, a few weeks later in early spring, one of the most horrifically violent acts in L.A. would occur at the Hoover plaza. A young African American woman was found stabbed, shot and completely burned. She was dumped in the large garbage bin in the rear of the apartment complex. Unlike most killings, this murder would draw national attention to the area, shining a light on the darkness that resonated in the Hoover Plaza.

It was painfully obvious that this environment was out of control. It had reached the breaking point for me. When an environment is out of control you must separate from it. As a community servant, I often offer this advice to youth and parents. If you cannot change the environment to make it better then you must leave to ensure your own safety and sanity.

After these two events, I was determined to get out of the immediate environment of 80th and Hoover and move closer to my school, Dorsey High on the west side. My first thought was to ask my uncle Charlie who lived near the area of Jefferson Street. My older cousin Andre had graduated from Dorsey two years prior and was now in college playing football for San Jose State University. So with Andre gone, maybe they would let me stay there to finish my senior year. However, it would have been a bit awkward to approach him being that I hadn't seen or spoken to either of them in years.

There were times that I wouldn't even have the bus fare to get back home, so I would crash at my best friend Daron's place who lived on Crenshaw and Adams not far from the school. He also had three brothers. There were five of them living in a two bedroom apartment. His father worked two full time jobs and wouldn't even notice when I would be there over night during the week. Mr. Patterson was a stern but fair dad but was too busy and too tired to keep up with his four teenage sons.

Daron and I were buddies since the 7th grade. We were always connected because of our initials DP. Every school registration listed us in alphabetical order so Deon Price and Daron Patterson were always in the same homeroom or assigned to sit near each other. We hung out and played hoops together for years. We took in a lot of street knowledge rolling up and down Crenshaw Boulevard. By the time we got to high school, we were known by everyone as the DPs along with Donnie Pumphry and David Phillips.

Darons mother passed away from cancer several years before we met. We were both being raised by single parents and both somewhat neglected. To escape the drama and stress of L.A., we would borrow Mr. Patterson's brown van and ride to the

Santa Monica Pier to chill out and do homework. We felt like we were on our own at times which created a bond between us. Little did we know that over a decade later, I would be asked to be the best man at his wedding.

As tight as we were, I knew I couldn't keep crashing at the Patterson *estate* on Crenshaw and Adams. I had to find some place soon. I was growing weary of ducking through alleys to get home and eventually I was going to have to confront the Hoover Street hoodlums. That moment came sooner than I expected. I was on my way home ready to do my usual Houdini act and disappear down the alley which I had done many times before. However, the timing was a bit off this time because the regular hoodlums that occupied the block caught a glance of me before I could cut down the alley. The urban survival manual says, never look like a victim and don't appear to be a threat. At this point it was too late for me to try to elude them and I knew they were looking eagerly at me because I was unfamiliar. My heart begin to race, anxiety was high but I could not show any outward signed of distress because they would definitely detect it. I had to think of something quick as I walked toward them. The closer I got to them, the more tense they appeared to me.

There was no way they were just going to let an unknown dude just walk through their hood. If this was a horror film which is what it felt like to me, you would hear that scary music at this point, like from the movie "Psycho". Before they could even approach me, I began to walk toward them directly. My survival instinct took over and I quickly became a customer looking for a quick drug fix. "Hey cuz, I need a couple of 20 sacks." Immediately there expression changed from attack mode to salesman. Although I was unfamiliar to them, they knew I was too young to be a narc or undercover cop so they were sold on me wanting to buy drugs. My next issue was the fact that I didn't have a dime to my name. They responded, "what you need cuz? I gotchu." My comeback was also instinctive, "Yeah, hold me five sacks, I'll be back with my stash." "You got it cuz, we'll be here." Whew! I just got a temporary pass and proceeded on my way home.

In my current occupation as a youth life skills coach, we talk a lot about listening to your instinct. As mentioned in the Omega Boys Clubs, *Alive & Free* violence prevention training for youth workers, you are trained to hear that inner voice or that scary music. In my life skills session a young man once commented, "You don't hear no scary music in real life". I encouraged him to really listen. You will hear your inner voice telling you something is about to happen and you better do something. That is that horror music giving you fair warning get the heck out before it's too late. I definitely heard the music that night near Hoover Street.

That quick thinking response probably saved my life but it was only a temporary fix. The next time they see me, they will be expecting me to buy 100 bucks worth of marijuana which was highly improbable. I could barely afford bus fare to get to school. I had to come up with something quick. My living situation was seriously effecting my concentration and focus in school. How could a kid concentrate on academics and completing homework when his biggest obstacle was making it home without being shot? Although there are some exceptions, the living conditions are the critical difference between successful and unsuccessful students.

CHAPTER 22

WEST SIDE

"My mother would shop for clothes in the same place we would get groceries."

My prayers were answered one Saturday night when my uncle came over to visit my mother. He invited me to attend his church on Sunday. We hadn't seen or heard from any of our extended family in several years. He had been a pianist for James Cleveland. Cleveland was a nationally known award winning gospel singer, arranger and composer who was also the pastor of the Corners Stone Baptist Church in Los Angeles. My uncle was a well-respected gospel musician in the L.A. Area. I hadn't been to church since my Grandfather who was also a Baptist minister, passed away in 1978. I had nothing to wear but a blue sweater and some jeans.

My uncle picked me up Sunday morning. The service was as the youth would say, *Hella* long like most black churches, but it was quite entertaining. The music was incredible, the singers were amazing. The choir was an awesome blend of overweight women with powerful voices and slightly feminine males with tambourines. My talented uncle directed it all from the seat of his black piano.

After church, he took me to Macy's department store which I have only seen from the outside. Macy's was one of those stores that was financially out of reach for me at the time. My mother would shop for clothes for me in the same place we would get groceries. Occasionally, we would go school shopping at Sears & Roebucks or Zody's department store. He had me try on several nice sweaters, jeans and outfits. I kept looking at the prices which annoyed him. He assured me to not be concerned with prices. "You aint paying for it so don't worry about what it cost. It aint none of your damn business." He snapped at me. Like my mother, he also had a very sharp tongue. He would curse anyone out whenever the wind would blow. He would be fresh out of church, bible in his lap and listening to gospel music but would curse out the next motorist for the slightest error on the road. His frequent and skillful use of the "B" word would make the rapper Too Short jealous. We left Macy's with clearly over $200 dollars' worth of clothes for me which was the most anyone had ever spent on me through my entire childhood.

Although I appreciated the shopping spree, the best thing my uncle did for me was to allow me to live with him for the remainder of my senior year. He had no idea what an impact this had on me. My living arraignments were my biggest concern and caused me a great deal of stress. He lived on the west side of L.A. near Leimert Park just off of Crenshaw Blvd. It wasn't Beverly Hills or even Baldwin Hills but I was definitely out of harm's way. I was also in walking distance from Dorsey High School

He owned a two story duplex in a quiet residential neighborhood. His home was decorated like a show room with leather furniture, Persian rugs and very expensive paintings. But, his prize possession by far was a beautiful pearl white Baby Grand Piano. It was in the center of the living room. He had it covered with a see through laced curtain. It was a beautiful display. One of the first things he said to me as he showed me around was "Don't touch my piano". It was that piano that drove my interest in learning to play music. I was taking music class in school but now my interest in learning to play music grew very rapidly.

Whenever he would leave, I would jump on that piano and play the hell out of it, just because he told me not to. I couldn't play worth a crap at the time but I would do my best Little Richard impression. I'd even play with my butt. After I had my fun on the piano I would take a damp rag and clean the entire instrument and wipe my fingerprints off.

Living with my uncle was an immense adjustment for me. He would periodically cook but most days we had fast food which was cool with me. I moved into his spare bedroom. It had a large console T.V. and a sofa bed. The best part was that it was about a 15 minute walk to my school campus at Dorsey High. I was at peace not having to dodge thugs and drug lords on the way home from school. It also gave me more time to relax and focus on school work which improved my grades almost immediately.

This further validates that the conditions of a child's home environment could either make or break him in terms of his educational progress. As a youth advocate, I use this experience as fuel to help reduce the high school dropout rate in public schools. If we can stabilize or improve the quality of life for as many youth and families, educational progress will improve. The only environment we really can control is our home. If there is no peace and consistency in the home, a young person could also suffer mental and emotional instability.

I was extremely grateful to my uncle for opening his home to me. He never married and had no kids of his own. The limited time that I lived with him I learned very little about him. We spoke sparingly and I never felt comfortable that he was at peace with the situation. During spring break, I went back to the Hoover Plaza to visit my mother. I had only been gone for about two months but my older sister who had two daughters, had already moved into my room. It was a two bedroom apartment so imagine how tight the conditions were.

After a week of the *unluxury* lifestyle of the Hoover Plaza, I was ready to head back to civilization at my Uncle's house on the west side. After spring break, I headed straight to school on Monday. My uncle had provided me with a key to the house so when school was out I walked to the house. When I arrived, I noticed that my key didn't work anymore. My uncle was not home so I waited by the stairs hoping he would arrive soon. As the sun set and darkness ascended, it became apparent that this was my Uncles' indirect way of saying that I was no longer welcome here. As the hours passed to beyond 7pm, I began to wonder where I would go if he didn't show. I had no bus fare to get back across town to the Hoover Plaza. There was no way of contacting them because my mother had no home phone. I'm cold, hungry and pissed off as to how I got into such a raggedy situation. Now I'm back into survival mode thinking of how I can get through this night without sleeping on the streets. I waited another hour or so to see if my uncle would be home soon. I even walked around the corner to the shopping center to see if I could use the phone to try to contact him. There was no answer. I left two messages. He was known to screen his calls by allowing the machine to answer while he listened. It was now nearly 9pm. He never showed.

My last option was to sleep in Leimert Park which would have been like spending the night in an actual jungle. At this time, Leimert Park was where crack heads, drunks, homeless people, gangs and drug dealers hung out. I quickly dismissed that thought and decided to take the 5mile walk down Crenshaw Blvd. toward Adams Street to crash at my buddy Darons' place. By the time I arrived, it was approximately 11pm. I was trembling cold, tired and hungry. He didn't even ask me too many questions, he just knew something was up and waved me in. He handed me a blanket and I slept on the floor. His older brother Mike would tease me often saying, "Damn, you are here more than my dad." The room was congested with three beds situated around each wall. As I dosed off, I came to the realization that at least for the time being, I was homeless. I stayed with Daron for a couple of days until I could get in touch with one of my sisters. My uncle never did answer my calls or contact me. I wouldn't hear from him again until many years later as an adult.

Although I appreciated the gesture of him allowing me to live with him even on a temporary basis, I resented the way he handled the situation. I was probably not the best person to live with at the time but I was always respectful and quiet. I even understood if there was a concern that I may have lost the key and someone could have gotten access to burglarize his home. He also knew that I had family members who were drug addicts at the time. Whatever the reason was for his actions, it played very loud to me at the time as yet another family member who let me down.

As I matured and became a father, uncle and mentor for youth, I vowed to become a resource and protector of young people who are in need. I decided to commit myself entirely to the welfare of children. My commitment and experience brought me to a crossroad that may have been similar to what my uncle faced with inviting a teenager like me into his home.

Many years later, I took in one of my teenage nephews. He was having trouble with what I thought was typical adolescent rebellion issues which was nothing that I was not prepared to handle. I had three kids including a teenage son and over ten years' of experience working with troubled youth in a Juvenile detention center. What was not communicated to me was that my nephew also had a serious drug addiction. I had moved him in to share a room with my younger son who was nine years old at the time. After several weeks we began to notice money being missing and strange behavior patterns. I decided to follow my instincts and search his room. What I found was disturbing for a 13 year old. I found several make shift smoking pipes that were made with Gatorade bottles and ink pens under his bed. The hardest decision that I had to make was to remove this boy from my home out of concern for my own children, which would prove to be a decision that I would later regret.

My nephews' life after that took a turn for the worse. Now he is an adult and is incarcerated at this time facing some serious felony charges. I second guess whether I gave up too soon on him. In my experience, I have provided material and training classes for parents and youth workers on "when to let go" and when to accept when you have done everything you can for a child.

When I arrived back to the Hoover Plaza where my mother and family was, the situation had deteriorated even more. My sister Cheryl had also moved in the apartment with all of her furniture. As I walked into the front door, I could barely move throughout the apartment. There was furniture everywhere. It was going to be a challenging two months before I graduate. I was more desperate than ever to complete by senior year and get the heck out of this crammed apartment, this drug-gang infested building, this violent neighborhood and the city of Los Angeles period.

The violence around me had not subsided. It had even reached what I thought was a safe haven, my school. It was the one place where I felt comfortable and at ease. I could freely express myself with no concerns for my physical wellbeing. Other than an occasional fight, it was pretty much a safe environment. That suddenly changed when fellow classmate, an honor student, Ernest Pickett Jr., was shot and killed in front of Dorsey High. There were over 200 witnesses present yet no one was either willing or able to identify the shooter. The street code at the time was that if you "snitched" you would suffer the same fate as the victim. It would be nearly 15 years before the perpetrator would be convicted for the murder. Ernest's death was difficult for the entire community. It devastated the students and tainted the once peaceful campus of Dorsey High School.

A second shooting occurred, this time on campus. A male student was in a confrontation with a rival gang member who did not attend Dorsey, was shot in the chest. He would eventually survive the injury but never returned to school. This was the beginning stages of the end of innocence on high school campuses in Los Angeles. School administrator decided to close the campuses during school hours which meant no one could enter or leave without permission. The presence of police on school grounds became a norm. Soon there would be metal detectors and random pat downs prior to students entering the campus. Things would never be the same. Urban high school campuses would soon resemble prison yards.

The next few weeks was filled with anxiety about what I will be doing after graduation and if I would even make it to June. I had no knowledge of the process of applying to college until my older brother, who had moved to the Bay Area in Northern California, guided me on who to contact. I was surprised to learn that it even cost $35 to even apply to a college. I spoke to a school counselor about my plans to apply to college in Northern California. He made my day when he was able to provide me with a voucher which waived the fee to apply. I made several photo copies of the voucher and applied to several Bay Area Universities, San Francisco State, San Jose State and Hayward State. Due to the instability in my current living situation, I always gave my older brother Herman's address in Compton, CA as my permanent address.

It would be Herman and his wife Jackie who would generously help me with other expenses such as the senior prom. Due to my bizarre home life, I had little interaction with girls. Having a girlfriend was out of the question. Although I was relatively popular at school as an athlete with a muscular physique and a charismatic personality, I was not confident enough to pursue any females at the time. I was simply too embarrassed to get involved with someone in fear of exposing them to my living conditions. Most guys were hustling and had material possessions that were attractive to girls. They had nice cars, jewelry, expensive clothes and pagers. I didn't even have a phone at home to contact a girl. My personal situation was just too raggedy to even try to get seriously involved with anyone. It wouldn't work out. Due to my popularity at school, many thought that I was quite a ladies' man. Little did they know that it was all a big front. I would avoid any serious advances from the ladies.

I learned the hard way with a failed relationship as a junior.

One of the most attractive females to me at Dorsey was Shelby. She was not popular because she was about her business. She stayed below the radar as far as school drama. She was not a part of any social group, sport athletic team or school activity. She kept to her one friend who was her home girl. They were always together during lunch or after school. She had beautiful natural features, smooth fair skin, light brown hair, very nice smile and big hazel eyes. She was classy and elegant but with a sweet yet urban demeanor. She was pursued by many but rarely gave anyone the time of day. We had third period biology together. I often teased her about the psychedelic colors she often whore. Before long we begin talking regularly after school before practice and soon we were making out after-school before practice. I would often call her from my brother Herman's house on the weekends. The official public notice that you were hooked up with someone was to have that person wear your jersey during game days on Friday. It was the official gesture that showed that you were that player's girl. So when I asked her to sport my number 14, it was official.

Deon & Shelby were a pair. Unfortunately, that relationship would be very short lived. After about a month she broke it off through a letter, stating irreconcilable differences, actually she conveyed to me that the relationship was just not moving. Could I blame her? We had not even gone on a date. I had no way of calling her and I was too embarrassed to invite her to my house which would have been a disaster. This would be the first and last time that I would engage in the experiment of dating, until I was out of L.A.

As I began to piece together my exodus from L.A., many of my friends were suffering casualties of the hostile environment. I begin to hear of more acts of violence that inflicted people close to me, including a child hood friend who we called Mouse. He was about my size with long braided hair. He was in and out of school due to his hustling and gang activity. We were connected due to his allusion that he could beat me in basketball. Our competitive nature often leads us to many black top battles on the court until he finally gave way to the streets. He lived near Jefferson Avenue where he was a part of the 20th street gang. He was even shorter than me so he did not make the Jr. Varsity team at Dorsey. I saw him sparingly in school until our senior year when he completely dropped out. I was not so surprised when I was delivered the unfortunate news that Mouse was shot and killed during a drug exchange. He was just 16 years old. To this day, I truly believe that if Mouse had made that J.V. Basketball team, he would still be alive today.

Around the same time, I learned of another classmate who was killed by an apparent self-inflicted gunshot. He was handling the gun while showing it to a friend when the gun went off killing him instantly.

These vivid tragedies amplify the need for positive productive activities and influences for young males during the adolescent years. Their social identity, self-worth and values are extremely critical during this time. In my profession, I have published many articles detailing the need for positive reinforcement for youth at risk which is all youth. "If youth are not involved in something positive, they will get involved in something." And that something, more than likely will lead them to incarceration or an early grave." For my brother Ronald and I, it was basketball that kept us out of harms way for the most part.

The last few weeks of my senior year was intense. I was very anxious about my future. I hadn't received any indication that I would be accepted into the colleges that I applied to. I did my best to focus on finishing my senior year without being suspended, expelled, arrested or shot. I avoided anything that could lead to trouble. I had my share of challenges on a regular basis. Just getting home safely was a difficult task for me while living in an urban war zone. June could not have come any sooner. I decided that whether I would be admitted or not by the three colleges I applied to, I was headed to Northern California. My older brother had moved to the Bay Area and encouraged me to begin the process of relocating to San Francisco.

Dorsey High class of 1986 consisted of a class of nearly 1000 graduates. To accommodate the super-sized class and their families, the ceremony was held at the Los Angeles Sports Arena. It was an iconic moment as it is for most individuals. It was an even greater accomplishment for me due to the extremely difficult conditions in which I had to endure during this time. Many of my closest friends were excited about finishing High school and spending a carefree summer in L.A. I did not share their enthusiasm. My motivation was simply getting the heck out of tinsel town. Three days after the graduation I did just that. Loaded with a meager backpack consisting of all of my worldly possessions, 18 years of my life, which was nothing but a pair of basketball shoes, some cookies and underwear, I boarded a greyhound bus from downtown L.A. headed to the Bay Area for the start of my adult life.

At my high school graduation with my mom and buddy Daron.

The only picture in the world with all 9 of us with mom

With my wife and kids. The latest shot of the Price family

Me . . . class of 1986 Dorsey High Grad

Me enjoying a training session with Bay Area youth

Delivering a youth employment development workshop

1962 The Gospel Metro-Tones with my
mother in the middle, top row

Me & Dr. Joe Marshall, Co-founder of the Omega boys club

At the MonStars of Motivation event with
Motivational Speaker Kevin Bracy

With my fellow Phi Beta Sigma brother,
Motivational speaker Wil Cason

Me in Jr. High Mt. Vernon Jr. High LA

In the early 60s Mom, Uncle Leon and Aunt LaVara

Classic shot of My Grandmother, Mother, Uncle and Aunt

Doing my life's work, reaching out to young males

CHAPTER 23

THE BAY AREA: A NURTURING ENVIRONMENT

". . . my lifes work and personal mission. "To improve the quality of life for the youth in our community"

During the summer in the Bay Area while living with my older brother, I was still a bit anxious about my immediate future. I had decided on a plan B if I would not be accepted by a University. I would enroll in a community college and look to transfer to one of the local four year schools. It would be a disappointment but at least I was prepared for it. Finally, in late July, I received acceptance letters from both Hayward State and San Francisco State University. I decided on S.F. State.

One of the first things I did when I settled on campus was pledge in a College Fraternity. The Brothers of Phi beta Sigma were very friendly and approachable. After the tense and strenuous pledge process I was proud to be a part of a nationwide brotherhood that stood for *culture for service and service for humanity.* One of the first community projects that I worked on with the brothers was mentoring teens in troubled areas such as East Oakland, Bay View hunters point in San Francisco and East Palo Alto. I was immediately impacted by the youth that I was working with who were experiencing the same issues that I had escaped in L.A. This work had such an empowering effect on me and the youth who I encountered, that I began to realize that this would become my lifes work and personal mission. *"To improve the quality of life for the youth in our community."*

During my educational activities, I was involved in a youth conference fund-raising event at San Francisco State University. This event would guide me to one of the individuals who would further inspire me to commit my adult life to youth work. I was asked to help with the theme of the event and to help accommodate our keynote speaker which included picking this person up from the hotel and bringing him to the event. I was a bit resistant due to the inconvenience of having to drive to the airport to a hotel and back to the college. I tried to delegate this detail to someone else but I was what they call a neophyte or "new blood" in the organization at the time. So, with a slightly tainted attitude and feeling like an "errand boy" I humbly preceded. When I arrived at the airport, I was still unaware of who this individual was other than his name. The name Geoffrey Canada meant nothing to me at the time other than a guy who was costing me gas money and time.

Part of my frustration was perpetuated by me driving the most raggedy car in the history of man. It was a Beige 1978 Honda Accord hatchback. Well, it wasn't really beige it was so rusty it looked beige. My drivers side door would not lock or close correctly so I had to hold it while I was driving. When I made a right turn the door would sometimes fly open. I could have been the first man to be ran over by his own car.

It was a 22 minute ride from SFO to the campus. By the time we arrived at the conference, I was schooled and inspired to the point that ignited a fire of passion for serving youth in me that would never be extinguished. I had never met anyone with such genuine commitment for saving and educating young people. Our exchange during that car ride was like me receiving a one on one basketball lesson from Michael Jordan.

During the conference as he delivered an inspiring key note speech on reducing youth violence in front of over a thousand people, he actually mentioned me and my experience in Los Angeles. Afterword he encouraged me to make a commitment to serving this population and to not waver. He signed my copy of his book "Fist Stick Knife Gun". I was 20 years old at the time and I have held on to that commitment to this day.

Geoffrey Canada (born January 13, 1952) has become a true American hero through his work serving underprivileged kids in the urban community. He is an American social activist and educator. Since 1990, Canada has been president and CEO of the Harlem Children's Zone in Harlem, New York, an organization which states its goal is to increase high school and college graduation rates among students in Harlem. He is a member of the Board of Directors of the After-School Corporation, a nonprofit organization that describes its aim as expanding educational opportunities for all students.

My career path would be made clear even more when I took a sociology class during the summer. The professor was a slightly built Afro centric senior professor who greatly resembled comedian/activist Dick Gregory. Dr. Zelty Crawford was extremely blunt and candid in his delivery with a strong militant mentality. With a PhD. From Stanford University, he was the head of Ethnic Studies at the College of San Mateo.

His style of teaching was very empowering and stimulated critical thinking. Whoever took his class was required to participate in a community service activity which was a part of their grade. The most effective project that we worked on was the Twilight youth program which was a youth crime prevention program that would continue for over ten years. Using basketball as the draw, we provided life skills education to at risk youth. My experience working community service projects with Dr. Crawford or "Doc Z" as we called him, cultivated leadership skills and a passion for community service that I still use to this day.

As a young volunteer youth worker at a community center I witnessed a physical confrontation between two relatively large males in their late teens. Several youth workers including myself made attempts to separate these two combatants who were engaged in an all-out brawl. We had a real challenge trying to separate them. Doc. Z who was in his mid-sixties and a very slim and frail grey bearded gentleman. He simply walked up to one of them and whispered something in his ear. The youth immediately begin to retreat and settle down enough for the staff to separate the two of them. It was amazing how such a simple gesture affected this young man. It was like he was given some sort of tranquilizer or sedative. What did he say to him? As my mentor, Doc. Z schooled me on how critical it is to establish a connection with the youth that you serve by making them believe that you are completely invested in their success. Oh, what he said to that youth is what I still say to youth today who may be headed in a dangerous situation, "You mean too much to me to get yourself hurt or in trouble." That simple statement could have a life changing effect on a person.

This inspiration would drive me into a successful career in youth services. I would do ten years in juvenile probation, another eight to ten in non-profit organizations to my current occupation as a youth career counselor. Throughout most of my adult life I have been fortunate to have helped to redirect and inspire at least two generations of youth throughout the state of California.

CHAPTER 24

FAMILY FULL CIRCLE

"Her presence is still the thread that links us together"

After 30 years struggling with drinking, my mother made a personal and spiritual choice to abstain from alcohol and has successfully maintained sobriety for 25 years. We constantly considered ourselves blessed to still have our mother with us in light of what she has endured in her 79 years. She gave birth to and raised nine children with very little help from our fathers. Besides her struggles, she managed to instill enough morals, ethics and divine wisdom to help guide each of us into responsible adulthood. The alcoholism lead her into the condition of high blood pressure, strokes, a knife attack, prison, third degree burns, an aneurism, emergency brain surgery and two hip replacements. She is honored and blessed with 29 grandchildren. We celebrate her love each year with a major family event. Her presence is still the thread that links us together. Besides experiencing the early stages of dementia, her sense of humor and charisma is still very obvious.

The Crowning of Debra Ann

Our family had been fortunate to have rarely loss someone close to us in my life time at the time. I knew the feeling of this particular morning felt odd when I received several missed calls from family members that I don't normally hear from but maybe once per month. My oldest brother Herman, who rarely calls unless he's on his way up here from L.A. also left me a cool but peculiar message to return his call ASAP. So, when I realized I had a call from him and three of my sisters, I knew something was wrong. Was it my mom who was often rushed to the hospital for having mild seizers? I was also concerned about my oldest sister Connie who had recently been diagnosed with Diabetes and was now on dialysis from a failed kidney.

I was at work at the time as a Youth Career Readiness Instructor for the Department of Labor, so I made an effort to maintain my composure. It was business as usual, until I checked my messages. The somber voice of my sister confirmed the dreaded news that no one wants to hear, "Deon, I'm sorry to have to leave you this message but . . . Debra Ann, passed away this morning . . . .".

My beloved older sister who had been separated from us since she was in her teens had taken sick over the last several months. We had not seen her since her return to California in 1999. It had been twenty two years since we had last seen her. It was as if it was a major family holiday. When we picked her up from the SFO airport, my brother Mike, our mother and I was nearly overcome with emotions.

That weekend we all spent the entire three days together. In fact it was the first time in over 25 years that all nine of us and our mother were together. Including each of our children and spouses, it was a total of 47 people as we invaded "The Home Town Buffet" in Stockton, California. After dinner, we stayed at my sister Cherolyn's house where we ate big, sang long and laughed loud. To this day it is considered one of our most celebrated family moments.

As I embraced the disheartening news, I was just returning from a ten minute break. My students were also returning to their seats from break. I was composed enough to not show any signs of distress. I was big on maintaining professionalism under any circumstance when working with youth. Although my heart was heavy with grief, I continued to deliver the lesson with the same charisma and energy as I normally do. By lunch time I had to take a brief walk near the water. I absorbed the cool natural air conditioning courtesy of the Bay, overlooking both the Bay Bridge and the Golden Gate Bridge from Treasure Island. After a moment or two of prayer and reflection, I contacted my manager to let him know that I would not be returning to the classroom due to a death in the family.

We began to make immediate arrangements to travel to Shreveport, Louisiana for the services which is where Debra spent the majority of her life. It is where she considered home and where she would be buried. The majority of her blood relatives were now on the west coast either Northern or Southern

California. The initial challenge was how most of us were going to make it out there 2500 miles away with the current travel expenses? The next most logical decision was to rent a couple of vans, pack a few items, load up and hit the road. Specifically highway 10 and head east.

Debra Ann Roberts, born February 1954, Shreveport, Louisiana. Talented gospel singer and Baptist church member. She worked with geriatric patients and senior citizens. She had one adopted daughter.

The first born, sister **Connie Roberts**; born in Shreveport, Louisiana, September 26, 1951. She graduated from Jefferson High school in Los Angeles with honors. She received an academic scholarship to the University of Montana. She has three adult sons, worked for AAA Insurance for nearly 20 years, retired and lives in Illinois. She is a very loving and nurturing person who basically helped raise all of her younger siblings. She is considered a second mother figure of the entire family. She has an amazing ability to win any argument instantly with the annoying pitch of her voice.

Herman Roberts III; Born in Shreveport, Louisiana, April 11, 1954, attended Lock High school; enlisted in the US Army as a Tank Crewman in 1974; Current occupation: AAA Insurance Information Tech; 33 years; resident Compton, CA; Raised three adult children one college graduate. He is responsible for everything I know about fatherhood, raising a family and to always be there for them. He and his wife Jackie(36 years), owns property in Compton, CA. Herman instilled in me that no matter how small a fellow is physically he can be big with respect in the eyes of his peers.

Cherolyn Howard; Born December 11, 1957 in Shreveport, Louisiana. Attended Jefferson High in Los Angeles, CA. She attended Los Angeles Trade Tech Community College. She majored in fashion design. She has six children, four of which are adults. Occupation: Substance Abuse Counselor; currently resides in Sacramento, CA. Cheryl is the most resourceful individual I know. Through her, I have learned to make something from nothing. No matter what the situation is, she can and will make a way. From bread pudding to sugar sandwiches she could make a meal from anything.

Ronald Omar Henderson: Born in Los Angeles, CA on March 1, 1965. Attended Crenshaw High School in Los Angeles, CA. Attended Compton College then transferred to Fresno State University on a basketball scholarship. He has two young daughters, owns property in Los Angeles with his wife of 18 years. His occupation is Production Assistant at Fox T.V. Ronald has framed my development as an athlete and coach and is responsible for my competitive spirit and sense of humor. To this day we would be in an environment and will find the humor in something without saying a word to each other while everyone else would be wondering what the hell we are laughing at.

CHAPTER 25

CURTAIN CALL

". . . this message that I intend to convey is the resiliency to survive and to overcome the circumstances of your environment . . ."

So here I am, the last born of Carrie Mae Howard, back on stage several years later this time in front of nearly 1000 people, delivering a dose of motivational comedy during a major event in Sacramento, California. The MC declares . . . "Ladies and Gentleman . . . put your hands together for the winner of the 'I am Greatness' spot light. Mr. Deon Price . . ." As I ascend to the stage to the inspiring cadence of the roaring appreciation of the crowd, also present in the audience is the source of my material and motivation for life which is my mother and my very own children.

Considering the many trials, emotional strain, hardships, headaches and heartaches endured by this family, here we stand. Besides the poor social economic circumstances, dangerous and impoverished living conditions, here we stand. Bear in mind that the tragedies, violence and substance abuse was not enough to overcome the strong desire to survive or to break that strong family bond. Against all odds this is an example of how you can reach beyond your circumstances to live a prosperous meaningful life regardless of your current situation.

The amazing lesson in this message that I intend to convey is the resiliency to survive and to overcome the circumstances of your environment through faith, humor, family and agape love. Our family story is not unique to the African American experience. It is more than likely a very familiar example that has occurred and is currently being experienced by people throughout our nation. What you experience in your current circumstances does not have to define you. How you handle every challenge, setback or obstacle that is in your path could also be the means to propel you to greatness. I often share with the youth whom I work with the quote from Mr. Charles Swindoll, "Life is 10% what happens to me and 90% how I react to it." This is a valuable life lesson in dealing with the tragedy and triumphs of the American family or as I like to call it, being "Raised in Hell".

ABOUT THE AUTHOR

Deon D. Price is a Youth Life skills Coach and former standup comedian with twenty years of experience as a Youth Service Worker as well as ten years in juvenile probation. He has dedicated most of his adult life to the field of youth and child development. Currently he is a Youth Career Transition instructor for the Department of Labor. Through his organization *Price Edutainment*, he has delivered motivational talks and seminars to parents, educators as well as students throughout California. His brand of motivational comedy is delivered with both humor and professional precision.

As a columnist, he has written weekly and monthly articles on the subject of modern youth culture in print and on-line. His Bi-weekly column *"This*

Generation" reaches several hundred thousand readers and has ran in several publications including the *Fairfield Daily Republic, The L.A. Sentinel, 311-Zine* in *San Francisco* and the *New York Times*. He also hosts an on-line web show of the same name.

Deon received the 2010 "I am greatness" spotlight award for motivational speakers. He also has appeared as a guest on Radio & T.V. programs to offer his unique perspective on issues regarding this generation of youth.

He has a wife and four children, three sons and a daughter. He lives in Northern California with his family.

CPSIA information can be obtained at www.ICGtesting.com
Printed in the USA
BVOW09s2241120214

344735BV00001B/1/P